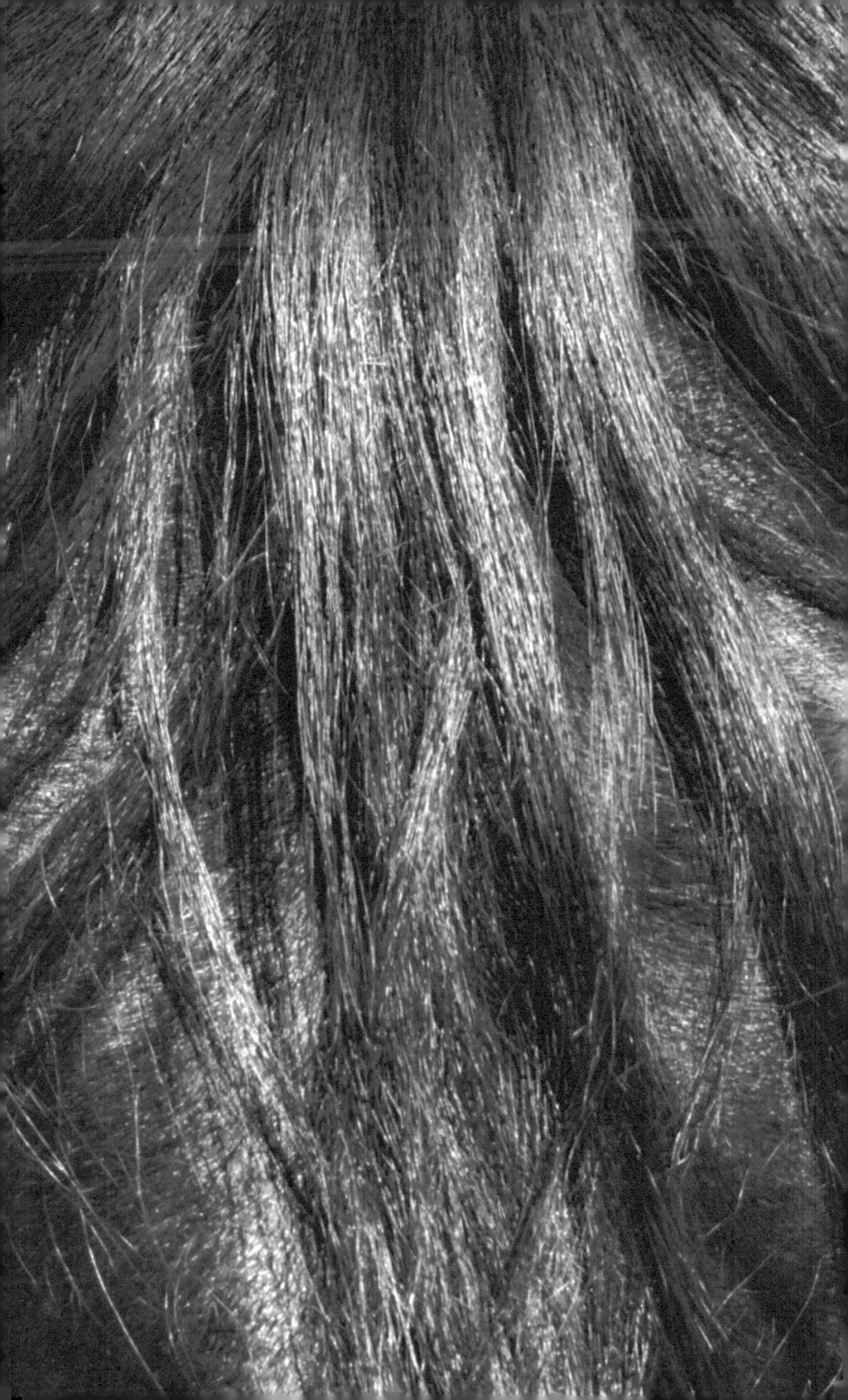

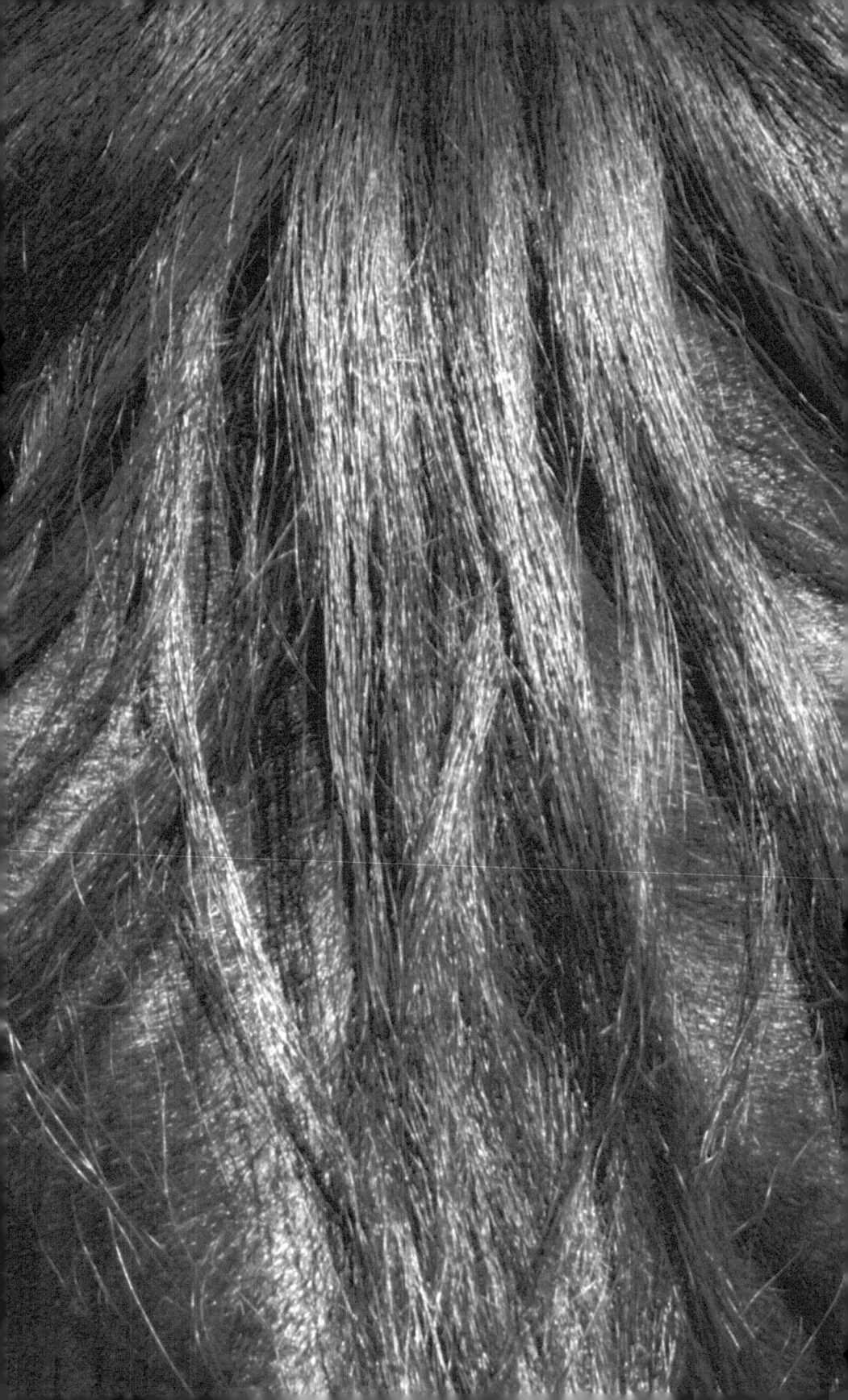

ADVANCE PRAISE FOR *RIDING FENCES*

"*Riding Fences* by mystery weaver, horse listener, and poet Christin Marie Staszesky is a stunning and absolutely unique body of work. I have neither seen nor read anything like it. This collection of memoir poems is not to be missed by anyone interested in the healing of intergenerational trauma, the healing between mothers and daughters, and especially the healing of childhood sexual abuse. The book is also an exquisite example of the dynamic potential of writing as an integrative healing modality.

"Christin's voice is original, courageous, powerful, and wildly authentic. Her brutal honesty is the direct reflection of her fierce commitment to her own transformational self-healing.

"Through Christin's radically creative poetic life review, she reminds us that 'to break the spell, you must tell.' Her poetry is her medicine, and she offers it to us as a profoundly important road map for the healing of these wounds. Finding her way back to herself through poetry and the body of a horse, her work is a potent source of insight and inspiration to those on the journey of healing, redemption, and reclamation."

—Diane Haug, MA, LPCC

Diane Haug, MA, LPCC, is a licensed mental health professional, a senior Grof Breathwork trainer and facilitator, and a founding director of the Grof Legacy Project in the US. She is an adjunct faculty member and mentor with the Center for Psychedelic Therapies and Research at the California Institute of Integral Studies in San Francisco, California, and has a long-standing relationship with

Southwestern College in Santa Fe, New Mexico. Among others, Diane has been a retreat presenter at Hollyhock Cortes Island, a retreat center in British Columbia, and Esalen Institute in Big Sur, California. Her current retreat offerings are focused between the beautiful Synergia Ranch in Santa Fe, New Mexico, and the magical Ocamora Retreat Center in northern New Mexico.

"As a survivor and a life coach who works with survivors, I take great delight in Christin's creative dance of words, bearing her heart, soul, and her body's experiences. I find her words touching my heart, soul, and body as well. Kudos for her courage and raw honesty."

—Rhea Maceris

Rhea Maceris is a life coach, hypnotherapist, and author of It's All About Me: Realizing I Am Enough.

"*Riding Fences* is both raw and tender. It is a powerful voice that speaks out boldly in the middle of what so often cannot be spoken.

"Trauma survivors enter into the process of healing wanting to forget. Staszesky's poetry and words dig deep into what needs to be remembered. This tender relating allows for the transformation the trauma survivor seeks.

"This poetic memoir is a beautiful and brilliant example exemplifying the dedication and tenacious spirit needed to embody the trauma-healing journey. Staszesky's own trauma recovery from childhood sexual abuse and her connection to her magical nonhuman allies, her horses, showcase the amazing creative power of trauma survivors."

—Manuela Mischke-Reeds, MA

Manuela Mischke-Reeds, MA, is a Hakomi psychotherapist and a founder of the Hakomi Institute of California. She is a trauma specialist and international teacher, offering her expertise to health professionals in the United States as well as New Zealand,

Australia, Germany, Colombia, Tanzania, Israel, and China. Manuela has worked with torture survivors from Latin America and Southeast Asia. She is the founder of Embodywise, a nonprofit professional somatic learning community. Manuela is the creator of ISITTA, the Innate Somatic Intelligence Trauma Therapy Approach, and the author of Trauma-Sensitive Movement: 96 Somatic Techniques to Support Nervous System Regulation and Embodied Transformation in Therapy.

"Christin Staszesky has shared her inner world of physical, emotional, sexual, and soul trauma with astonishing honesty and profound creativity. She has taken on self-healing with depth and integrity using her gifts of creativity in poetry, dreamwork, and the equine path. Her lifelong love of horses, riding, and nature were inspired by a mother who, as a vulnerable human herself, both fails and works to repair her relationship with her daughter over the course of decades. This is a book about the sometimes harrowing hard work and lifelong commitment that true healing, not just surviving, requires. Her ladder of angels, so beautifully rendered, includes beloved horses, therapists, guides, and the inner wisdom of the psyche. Christin finds self-compassion and self-blessing—the great gift, the treasure hard to find."

—Penelope Tarasuk, PhD

Penelope Tarasuk, PhD, is an IAAP Jungian psychoanalyst, fellow fence rider, artist, and author of Polishing the Bones, *a Jungian story of a woman artist working with her dreams through her dying.*

"Exquisitely crafted and profoundly revelatory, the poems in this volume offer an account of sexual trauma and its effects from the inside. They describe the triumph of truth-telling, and the spirit and support that enable healing.

"*Riding Fences* is an intimate account of the experiences of confusion, fragmentation, and frozenness that such violations engender and will be invaluable for those impacted by sexual trauma and those who support them.

"Indeed, a resurrection occurred through the writing of this account; as a therapist and Grof Breathwork facilitator privileged to witness the healing that is possible despite horrific experiences such as those described here, I find myself awed by the beauty of these poems. And I am graced to count their author as a friend, and to have witnessed her transformation and re-empowerment."

—Pamela Stockton, MA

Pamela Stockton, MA, is a licensed professional clinical counselor practicing in New Mexico. She is a somatic experiencing practitioner working with trauma clients. Pam also holds juris doctor and master of theological studies degrees.

"I am moved, shaken, and in awe of this utterly unique offering to the world. It can't be put in a box—deeper than a memoir, more than a story, beyond poetry. I don't believe anything has existed like it before. You will weep, hold your breath, laugh, shout, and have to put it down at certain moments. Fearless. Raw. Wise. Exquisite. This is a journey of revelation and redemption, including resources and guidance for everyone's healing. Unforgettable."

—Amy K. Musson, MA, PCC

Amy K. Musson, MA, PCC, is a growth and leadership coach, depth seeker, both-and thinker, mind expander, and host of The Growth Moment *podcast.*

Riding Fences

ALSO BY CHRISTIN MARIE STASZESKY

5 days: A Lifetime of Love in Seven Thousand Two Hundred Minutes

A Memoir

Riding Fences

poems from the crossed
country of my body

Christin Marie Staszesky

Light Rider Press

Riding Fences: poems from the crossed country of my body

Copyright 2025 by Christin Marie Staszesky

All rights reserved.

No part of this publication may be reproduced, stored in a retrieval system, or transmitted in any form or by any means, electronic, mechanical, photocopying, recording, or otherwise, without written permission of the publisher.

Published by Light Rider Press, Houston, TX
www.thelightrider.com

Edited and designed by Girl Friday Productions
www.girlfridayproductions.com

Design: Paul Barrett
Project management: Abi Pollokoff
Editorial production: Katherine Richards
Cover photography by Rodney Bursiel
www.rodneybursielphotography.com
Endsheets photo © Shutterstock/Abramova Kseniya

ISBN (hardcover): 979-8-9985542-0-9
ISBN (ebook): 979-8-9985542-1-6

Library of Congress Control Number: 2025906911

First edition finalized May 2024

*To all survivors.
Everywhere.*

In the United States, someone is sexually assaulted every 68 seconds.[1]

And every 9 minutes, that someone is a child.[2]

The age range of these child victims is most often between 12 and 17 years old.[3]

Sexually abused children know their abuser over 90 percent of the time.[4]

An estimated 1 out of every 4 girls in the United States experiences child sexual abuse.[5]

---

1. https://rainn.org/statistics
2. Ibid.
3. https://rainn.org/statistics/scope-problem
4. https://protectyourchildren.org/eye-opening-statistics
5. https://www.cdc.gov/child-abuse-neglect/about/about-child-sexual-abuse.html#cdc_behavioral_basics_quick-quick-facts-and-stats

CONTENTS

Foreword xix
Preface xxiii
A Reader's Guide xxvii
    The Truth Is 3
    Alphabet⁺ 4
    Six Weeks Old 7
    Grandmother⁺ 9
    I Was 13 13
    How Can 15
    Blue Laces⁺ 16
    Dad 18
Herd Medicine: Dear Teddy 23
    So I Do 27
    Abuser Erasure⁺ 32
    Your Eyes 33
    Living Room Picnic 35
    Hawk⁺ 40
    A Different Story 45
    Queen 47
    Dyad 51
Herd Medicine: Dear Misty 55
    Abdication 59
    His Arms 62
    Cutter⁺ 63
    Mane 66
    Unaware 69
    After You Left⁺ 74
    12 Steps 77
    Grandstand⁺ 80

⁺Denotes additional details and insights found in Poem Notes.

Herd Medicine: Dear Bobby 85
    While Castrating Bull Calves⁺ 89
    White 93
    Hypervigilance 94
    Celibate 97
    Bad Therapy⁺ 99
    I Warned You 104
    Before Sleep Comes to Take Me 105
    In My Hair 108
Herd Medicine: Dear Smoke 111
    The Colliding Body 115
    Doctor's Office 116
    Good Therapy 117
    What Abuse Does to Your Marriage 121
    What I Couldn't Say 124
    Here I Am at 48 129
    Realization 131
    Me (Too) 133
Herd Medicine: Dear Royal 135
    Height of a Horse Is Measured in Hands⁺ 139
    A Chorale of Silence⁺ 142
    This One I'll Keep 149
    What Prevented You from Rescuing Me⁺ 152
    Wish⁺ 157
    The Year I Collected Dolls 158
    Cards 164
    Migraine⁺ 165
Herd Medicine: Dear Wren 173
    South Texas Lazarus⁺ 177
    I Am Not 187
    It Was Prearranged⁺ 188
    Apple 190
    Fireflies Flashlights and Horned Toads 192
    Pancakes⁺ 200
    Citizen 202
    The Fifth⁺ 206

Herd Medicine: Dear Mission	207
What If I'd Become a Cherry Clerk⁺	211
Stay	214
Sober	225
A Collection of Love Letters	227
Breathwork	230
The Price	236
Homage to My Heartbreak	241
Empty Chair⁺	242
Herd Medicine: Dear Cicero	247
A Thousand Tongues⁺	251
Basic Instinct	253
Mother, Who We Have Become⁺	259
The Peony Key⁺	264
Road Map	270
Amor Fati	274
Elegy	279
Who Am I	281
Epilogue	293
Postscript⁺	297
Letter to Survivors	299
Resources	307
Poem Notes	323
Gratitude	331
About the Author	337

FOREWORD

Embarking on Christin Marie Staszesky's memoir, *Riding Fences: poems from the crossed country of my body*, one begins a journey into a declaration rarely voiced with such raw honesty. Through her poetry, Staszesky confronts a reality many face, yet few discuss openly—the shadows of sexual abuse. She guides us through a path of realization and confrontation. From the very first poem, it becomes clear we are not merely readers but witnesses to a profoundly personal truth.

Staszesky's artistry lies in her ability to make "you feel something inside," a feat she achieves with striking immediacy and intimacy. Her poems are not just read; they are experienced. As she dives into the privacy of her pain, exploring and expelling it in the public gaze, the reader is inevitably reminded of their own. This dichotomy between private suffering and public sharing creates a powerful, purgative effect. Ready yourself. This book may reveal parts of yourself beckoning for the light of truth.

The essence of Staszesky's work transcends traditional poetry. She offers messages of truth, pain long repressed, and confusion finally given voice. Through a unique blend of stanzas, meter, letters to equine guardians, and raw emotion, she reconnects both herself and her readers with experiences that previously lacked words. This collection is not just an anthology of poems; it is a narrative of reclamation, revelation, and the universal truth of human suffering.

FOREWORD

At one point in the text she becomes a centaur—a creature both grounded and mythical—symbolizing her role as a guide from the external world into the depths of interior landscapes. As a creator and a healer, she invites us to reexamine what has been hidden and encourages the expression of buried truths necessary for healing. Speak it. Write it. Reveal it. Her reflections on the nature of trust and relationship, illustrated through her interactions with horses, resonate deeply, underscoring the themes of strength and empowerment amidst vulnerability.

Riding Fences is a masterful exploration of depth, pain, violations, confusion, abandonment, neglect, and most importantly, resurrection and redemption. It serves as an invitation to engage in a ritual of expression, uncovering hidden or concealed parts of ourselves that need to be voiced. Staszesky's bravery in revealing her truths offers a beacon for others to follow, prompting a personal journey into the dark roads of one's inner landscape.

In a poignant reminder, Staszesky brings us to the realization that we all carry silent pains, often masked behind smiles. Her book acts as a call to action, urging us to recognize the healing power within and the importance of acknowledging the burdens many bear silently. Through her poetic journey, she exemplifies the transformative power of creative expression, guided by the inspiring words loosely attributed to Carl Gustav Jung: "I am not what happened to me, I am what I choose to become." This collection is a testament to the strength found in vulnerability and the infinite capacity for love at the core of human existence.

Christin Marie Staszesky's *Riding Fences* is not just a book of memoir poetry; it is a call to healing, a reminder of the resilience of the human spirit, and an invitation to embark on a journey of self-discovery and redemption. It challenges us to confront our truths, to embrace our pain, and ultimately, to find solace in the shared experiences that unite us all.

Amor fati!

> —John W. Price, PhD, LPC, is a depth psychotherapist, cofounder of the Center for Healing Arts and Sciences in Houston, Texas; president of the board at the Jung Center, Houston, Texas; creator and host of *The Sacred Speaks* podcast; and is on the faculty of Esalen Institute, Big Sur, California.

PREFACE

Three years ago, I awoke with a Pandora's box of a dream.

I am in a tight-knit cityscape. Placed among the skyscrapers, there is a large corral with a brick gate. The gate suddenly swings open and all of my horses come charging out at once. A thought bubble floats momentarily above them: "We have always kept your secrets."

I wake up.

That morning, while doing my ritual writing and making an entry about the night's dream, I was surprised by a burning question I had just written down. "What am I going to do about it?" I felt upheaval. It catapulted me toward the idea of this book and bringing it all to light. It was a stars-in-the-sky idea, but suddenly I found myself looking up, after a long time of looking down.

I began weaving on that cosmic loom, piecing together the first threads of a vision for this collection. Was I finally ready to write about what happened? Because it was definitely all still inside me and thrashing around louder and louder. Just like a horse I once owned who wouldn't stop kicking the barn.

I decided to enroll in a ten-day writing retreat to focus this vision. I figured that even if I chose not to pursue this inkling, this urge, then I would at least use the time to sharpen my writing skills.

PREFACE

On the morning before the retreat, a snake appeared on my doorstep. I saw him even before my dog did. I spotted the black-and-gold herringbone pattern on his shiny skin as the early morning sun glowed on it. He was stretched out, arrow straight, right at the foot of the steps to my porch. He was unmissable.

In the five years that I have lived on this two-acre country property, I have never seen a snake, not one, and this is Texas. He got my attention, and it was right on time.

I signaled my dog, Lali, to wait; I didn't want her bitten. Then I stood very still on the top step, looking down at the snake. As I watched him, with his tongue flickering, I started wondering about the symbol of a serpent. What was the message that had come to me in this quiet light?

Transformation. Change. Readiness. Death. Medicine. An arrival at a point of departure. A point of no return. Poisons. Antidotes. Directions. Decisions. I thought of the caduceus. The emblem of a snake wrapped around a walking stick, the symbol of peace and healing. It is also the magic wand carried by Mercury, the messenger of the gods. As the snake slithered slowly away into the grass, I remembered he is also embedded in the sacred staff of Asclepius, god of medicine and dreams. This dream god was raised by a centaur and could bring people back from the dead. I felt a shiver of convergence.

Was this a response to the questions that had begun to haunt me? *Is it time to write my story? Am I ready to tell the truth?*

That morning I received my answer. It was a go-ahead for this project, a cosmic high-five, a cracking open of my biggest box of unfinished business, the descent into the basement of my soul to gather up all those banished parts of me. I was the one, the only one, who could bring those stories out of the doom and into the sunlight. It was time. My heart knew it. And the message had arrived in a way I couldn't miss.

The next morning was day one of the writing retreat. Before the class began, I walked barefoot in the grass, holding a steaming cup of kukicha green tea. As I listened to the day rising, my feet stopped themselves and I looked down.

There, at the tips of my toes and completely intact, was the herringbone skin of my messenger.

A talisman of my readiness, from the dream god himself, lying at my feet.

I set my cup down at the base of an oak and gathered the gift into my hands, releasing it gently here and there from the grass. The skin, so freshly shed, was soft and oily. Malleable. Ready for change and reshaping. I knew then that I would be brought back from the dead, changed and reshaped when the words spilled out of my body. I was ready to shed my old skin, which had grown too tight. I was ready to begin.

Riding Fences is my journey of recovery from childhood sexual abuse. Like a rider on horseback, following a fence line for miles to see what needs to be repaired, these poems helped me discover and make an inventory of all the places of me that had been damaged. Ruptured. Torn. Trespassed. Trampled. Hurt. And how the sun came to shine on those now mended places. It is a metaphor for the healing of my body and reclamation of my soul.

I am a lifelong horsewoman. I have been from the moment my mother put me on the back of a horse for the first time when I was only weeks old. As she rode regally upright in the saddle, I rode her strong back, hugged close and secured in a pack. I learned that the back of a horse is a sacred place of initiation that offers a vantage point not commonly seen by mere mortals.

Over the years, as I rode the fence line of my body and healing journey, I came to understand that we carry all the tools and supplies needed to repair the ruptures inside us and along the skin lines of our own bodies.

At times my experiences on this journey have been solo, but at different times I have done this work in the company of others. Sometimes

PREFACE

I carried tools tied to the saddle. And sometimes the supplies I needed were carried and offered by others. Almost always, we need that extra pair of hands to shine a light, pull that wire, hold the post, dig the hole and fill it in. Sometimes what's needed is simply for someone to hold our hand while we stand and weep at the damage.

And always, to point the way home.

Horses and poetry have been the air I have breathed since my beginning. These two passions have traveled with me along the fences that have traced every year, every moment of my life.

I write as a way to understand and make sense of my being-ness, humanity, and what's happening around me and inside me. I came to use poetry as a way to lessen my deepening isolation, both as a child and as an adult. Poetry became a balm to my ever-present, unexplained sense of urgency, a close companion to my confused and lonely self. The pen and pencil became my instrument of reconstruction and resurrection. Graphite and ink replaced the threat of blood.

Poetry and horses are good medicine.

So turn these pages, ease into your saddle, and ride with me along my fence line. I hope it will empower you to discover your own. For those of you who are survivors, you will read these poems and recognize a sister who understands.

Thank you for reading my words, my poetry, and allowing me to touch a moment of your life.

May you bask in the splendor and the beauty that is the miracle of your own existence.

Christin Marie Staszesky
May 2024
Houston, Texas

A READER'S GUIDE

Dear Reader,

As you embark on this journey, I invite you to read slowly and to care for yourself. Although you may choose to, this story is not intended to be read in one sitting. You might find that you need to curb your speed, ride the fence line gradually, and allow the poems to settle and land with some time and breath in between.

Some of you may find yourself wondering if I am OK. I can assure you that yes, I am. You can allow that kind caregiver part of yourself to relax, as I am on the other side and feeling unmistakably solid and stable.

Here you will find a few tips for self-care, if you discover that the collection ignites too much impact, or triggering sensations, for the moment at hand:

- Give yourself permission to read slowly, even very slowly. Perhaps only one poem at a time.
- Give yourself permission to stop reading.
- As you read, as needed, ground yourself by placing one hand on your own body, your arm, your chest, or the side of your cheek.
- Go for a brief walk. Or a long one.
- Be cozy and bring comfort to yourself. Wrap a blanket around you and have a hot cup of tea.

- Write. Have your journal nearby to make notes or to record your reflections, questions, and thoughts. Feel welcome to write in the margin of the book itself.
- Check for your own safety. Make sure you are safe as you read.
- Ask for support from a trusted loved one or friend.
- If you are a survivor, perhaps consider reading this collection with your therapist.

At the back of the book, I offer an extensive section of resources, including an SOS Tool Kit that you can find on page 308. You may choose to read or review that section first. Feel free to highlight which resources feel available to you right now. Lean on them or others you already have in place.

Lastly, if you don't feel ready to read this collection, perhaps it's not the right time, and that is OK. You have permission to set this book aside for another day. Or forever.

You caring for yourself, as I have cared for myself, is my central interest and concern. It looks different for each of us. Every way, is more than OK, and welcome.

Keep breathing. Here we go—let's ride together.

Christin

The cost is nothing less than everything.

—T. S. Eliot

THE TRUTH IS

each of my cells

is cleaved in aloneness

needled back roughly

with horsehair twine

tattered prayer ribbons

dotted with tear speared stars

and the belief

I will die

with my heart

unbeat

skin

unseared

by the kiss of my own

desire

ALPHABET[+]

angry, after, absence, abandon, adultery, anxiety
A is for abuse down by the sea.

boy, beach, blue couch, burn, bullets, bottle, boss, brass monkey
B is for breasts too young to touch.

cut, cunt, cries, covert, chainsaw, cop, child
C is for candy, a nun friend visiting my mother, once driving us, you asked if she liked to be licked or sucked.

dog, dance, date, daughter, dawn, dick, dangerous, dissociate, depression
D is for dirty and never coming clean.

escape, embarrassed, elephant, effexor, ego
E is for evil and how it followed me.

finger, fuck, father, fear, fragmentation, flashlight
F is for fences, the ones they all crossed.

gun, girl, guts, gag, groom, grief
G is for gross and what my body tells me I am.

horse, high school, hawk, hide, humiliate
H is for help and how it never came.

isolation, insomnia, insecure
I is for I-don't-know, the answer my teacher gave when I asked why everyone looked the other way.

jerk, jealous, justify
J is for the jungle I am lost within.

kiss, kick, kneel, klonopin
K is for knife that I keep in my purse.

loser, lover, larry, late, lithium, lure
L is for lock when you said *you aren't going anywhere.*

mormon, mother, migraine, mistake, my sharona, memory, molester, married man
M is for muffled, my whimpers under your hand.

neck, noise, never, night-lights, nightgown, neighbor
N is for no which means yes in their world.

overt, open window, "oh, it's you," obedient
O is for oh my god this can't be true.

pussy, penis, payne, punch, pry, pressure, prozac, predator, prey, ptsd
P is for pain and how much a person can take.

queen, quiver, quiet
Q is for quaint which this story is not.

rape, razor blade, ruin, rubber band, run, registered sex offender, ridicule
R is for remains and how much is still left.

stadium, shame, slice, seventh street rooms, sex, stalker, sand castle, sand pile, slap, secret
S is for steal and what you took from me.

tom, trash, trailer, trust, touch, tears, tim, time, torment, terror, trauma
T is for tragedy and all I went through.

underwear, underneath, underage, unseen, undone
U is for unearth and how to locate missing pieces.

virgin, victim, violence, violent, violate, viper
V is for vermin, those people who hurt children and animals.

writer, welbutrin, walk-in, why, woman, wail, worn, water, want
W is for weak and that I am not.

expectations, experience, exchange, excruciating
X is for example, the one I never had and the one I hope to leave.

yuck, yell, yield, yoga, yellow impala, yellow heart, years
Y is for yes, the one I never gave.

zero, zoloft, zipper, zombie
Z is for zeitgeist that allows children to be abused by adults entrusted in care.

SIX WEEKS OLD

the day I stopped listening
to her heartbeat

the day I started to hear
the heartbeat of hoofbeats

I have no active memory of it
it was retold only later

the ribbed royal corduroy blue
baby backpack she wore
that swaddled me safe
against her warmblooded lithe
and young sinewy back
on that first initiation ride

hangs now still
in the back of the hall closet
next to other castoffs
puffy vests marked with dried tattoos
from muddy dogs feet
horse mouths full of grain

camo jackets with small bulges
left in the pockets
old spent shells
their casings empty

the go-to barn coats worn by all
mom

me
visiting friends who want to help feed
the novelty allowing them not to care
what they wore

I have her memory of how I became
so quiet and still
she thought I was sleeping
the four beat rhythm lulling me
the steady clops of u-shaped
eon hardened hooves
ribbon smooth vibration
echoed through my fresh formed
baby bones as soul bones
turned the great gold wheel
etching out our marrow
with shared DNA
the nick and scar of time

going by

gone by

I wasn't asleep

I was listening

GRANDMOTHER⁺

who told me
one day
I'd write poetry
of my own

wrote me
a poem once
and sent it with her face

with only a few gestures
her face-words
spelled out each sound
for me to hear

scribbled up eyes
cut side and diagonaled-down
her upper lip inch wormed up
to show her teeth
wavy highways in her forehead
caused an accident inside me

I'd been fresh from the shower
hair still wet
slicked and
combed smooth
wearing my dad's v-neck

hanes
white teeshirt

I plopped down
in front of her
on the floor
all ankles crossed
and knees out
the hem of my top
stretched straight across my thighs
it was the edge of a cliff
she faced

she threw her
drawn hard poem
at my feet
and barked
her gut at me

"Close your legs!"

then she got up
and walked away

I knew it was
a poem
because they say

a poem
makes you feel
something inside

what I felt
was so big
a rung bell broke
my small chest
in two

I could not contain it
it bloomed out
of my heart
the pink petals
creeping slowly
up my neck
to lodge
in my cheeks
seeping water sluiced
my eyes

there were no more words
but I got the meaning
without needing
to ask an adult

between my legs was gross

in the kitchen I could smell
my favorite mom-popped-stovetop
popcorn popping

it was movie night
and the never ending story
was just
beginning

forty years later

I realized what had cooked my cheeks
to that ruddying red way back
that evening of the movie

when she'd looked and saw
under the edge of me

it was her own boiling body's
decomposed embarrassment
roiling her alive

it was never mine

I was ten

I WAS 13

sitting on the top step
waiting
my face turned right to the street
wringing my hands
touching my braid
bark brown
his car wheels never touched
the sharp gravel of the drive
idling in park, the car not coming close
clear and away from the house
no one home but me
watching him swagger
stalking towards me
steel toes crunching
his white hard hat
still pasting his hair flat

when our eyes finally meet
he's so near all I can see
is the coffee cream floss
of his upper lip
inside my head
I pray
I beg

please leave, please go
pay attention
I'm lost
find me

he feels grown I feel small
hearing my voice whisper "hi"

he was 21

HOW CAN

a child
embody her budding body clothes
smelling blossom clean
and new of sensuality
when all she has to choose from are
moth eaten
torn
frayed
too tight
buttonless
zipper-less
sex suits
in size woman
or eve

BLUE LACES[+]

flash

racing down the empty hallway

echoing the vacancy

bursting me at the seams

I hurl my curled fist

fat with the currency of rage

into the yellow field of lockers

scraping open my scab picked misery

the sound shears away

any last wisp of gravity or ground

his ironed smooth, stone blue suit

rounding the corner, pulling up short

his lips, in open 'o' shock

I swallow vinegar ichor

wrench and sew back together

into a ripped and jagged smile line

the ugly wet maw of my mouth

I hide the staining

of shadow blue lacing

blossoming across split right knuckles

behind my back

DAD

we didn't pack you sandwiches and snacks
we didn't hold you tight
we didn't wave goodbye
we didn't cry

we didn't even know you'd left

you never closed the door behind you
but left it standing open wide
I wonder if you hoped
we would come and join you
or that one day you might return

but that open door
that's how they all came rushing in
like the gulf lapping up the frilly shoreline
and every single thing inside it

beach weekends were the family favorite
everything went into the truck
shovels and buckets and toy cars and ice
books and towels
sunscreen and hats
frisbees and footballs
flipflops and kites
us and mom
everything all
except the peanut butter and jelly sandwiches
left forgotten on the counter
never making it into the cooler

at lunchtime we'd groan in mock complaint
and happily munched
on watermelon grapes and cheese crackers

a middle afternoon game we both loved to play
you'd put me up high on your shoulders
you used to keep me from them
and I'd laugh and you'd laugh
when the ocean would wash out
its own language against us
the encoded white water script
concealed inside the wave crest tops
visible yet unreadable
was a future message that spoke
to the erasure of our bodies

drenching us again and again
inking your hair black
your wet curls matching mine

don't let them get me dad
I've gotcha Chris

I stand on the shore on my own feet now
I keep my own self dry dad
and crazily
I still love this beach

even though I met one of them there
you wouldn't have known that
all of us kids that day with mom
strolling and shuffling ourselves on the sand
having been too rowdy and sullen at home
she loaded us into the car
and we drove the familiar back roads
to the place we'd always gone
as a family before

we hung ourselves out the windows
like dogs
our skin tongues and noses drinking
the balmy salt wind
its umami spinning charms on us
mile by mile getting closer
our woes and irritations
transformed into kite-high glee
the one place we all loved to be
we tumbled out of the car
before it was even fully parked
headlong we'd fly for the surf
mom yelling after us to be careful
and watch out for your sister

which one?

hours later after we'd poured out our angst
and grown more sane
if not up
we'd beachcomb for shells and sea glass
only picking it up if it was ready
the edges worn smooth

we saw this brawny man
hair dyed blond without companion
scraping and shoveling
erecting sand castles
mom said I should go talk to him
and so I did
you weren't there dad

decades later
on this same sand
I'm bathing my feet
the water washes them clean
ablution mystery

apologies for all that's been lost
and what was born in your absence
lifetime of misharbored shame
racked up to my knees

when the water washes back to sea
it takes my stains out deep
into its gulf belly where no light gets
no hands touch
marking me clean
forging my body safe again
for itself

so goes the water dad
so goes the salt
and so go these sorry spells
that were written and cast
written and cast
under the shadows of five
different hands

I remember it was famously you
who always
prepared those silly peanut butter sandwiches

the jelly smudges and peanut buttery fingers
beloved by us all
salt tinged with beach

and you who always left them

until that day you didn't anymore

HERD MEDICINE

Dear Teddy,

My mom told me you were so wild they had to round you up with dirt-bike motorcycles to be able to catch you. They told her she was crazy for choosing you. But she saw something special and different in you and told those men, "You don't know my daughter, this pony is the one." So I received you, a wily Shetland pony with a red ribbon braided through your mane for my fifth birthday. And that was the day that I became a centaur.

It was the same year *The Black Stallion* came out. The fourth time I saw it in the theater, I sat next to my granddaddy. I barely touched my popcorn for ecstatically announcing to him moment by moment what would happen next. He shushed me gently and invited me to whisper it all into his ear instead. That post-movie neck crick must have been fierce, and yet our face-full grins surely told a different story.

It didn't matter day or night, what clothing, shoes or no shoes, saddle or no saddle, we could be found flying across the pasture, your hooves tearing up the yard or eating up the pine-covered woods. Our feet never touched the ground. My white nightgown, so often still warm from sleep, serving as wings catapulting us across the very sky.

The times you came back without me instilled no fearful meaning. I'd leap back onto your back in a flash, and off again we'd go. Teddy, I taught you to rear on command. And when I'd call for you, you'd come running, your tail a ripe wheat bronze, whipping full sail behind you. The untold hours parading by would blow kisses at us. Their cheeks pink with puffed satisfaction at our blissed oblivion. Those minutes to hours to days to weeks to years I spent with you were perfectly landed smooches that budded and burst into blooms. I was too young to name them as the gifts they were: The first true template of belonging in a world beyond a warm, watery, loving womb. The first feel of independence. The joy of responsibility. I loved you without measure.

You followed me from Madawaska, Maine, all the way to Olympia, Washington. My daddy had you shipped cross-country because I could not bear being separated from you. You planted seeds of resilience with your rugged little Shetland body, deep into the fertile soil of my carefree early childhood. You sequestered them there, into my body, where they would remain in the dark loam of silence, until later.

Thank you for initiating me into your world. You were the first.

Love,

Christin

SO I DO

in the dark you tell me to lay down

I do

the bed undulates underneath me

rippling until I'm still

a first of many

I already know I don't like it

you say to close my eyes

I do

my own body, a solitary confinement

betraying me

trapped inside a double darkness

I begin to shake

these blankets and sheets

don't belong to me

I am a foreigner here, unwelcome

you'd had me come

concealed through the back door

led me by the hand

yours swallowing mine

up the rickety stairs to the right

past your cramped kitchen galley

last night's leftovers

dirty rice and beans, harden in silence

from the countertop

a bottle of brass monkey

eyes me all the way into your room

you point to the bed

I lie down

you say to open my arms

I do

all at once I

disappear into black

and electrify

with my cells like bells

tolling screams I can't hear

unable to tell if there are a million

ants or just two hands

traipsing over my ghost cold skin

you can trust me

my body behaves

quivers like I do

but I know I don't

your words-sound slit my shroud

my lungs are guppies

gasping on sand

I slam back to track

your fingers

my clothes do not protect me

no matter how tight

your touch rough then lewdly

feathering my crawling skin

I am prison snared

my frozen shadow

sweats and shatters I search

for your other hand

I can't tether it

I shrink from the surface

needing to drown

down into your bed

a septic marsh, oozing bile

your fingers trawl, too slowly

down the side of my chest

over the young bump of my breast

smothering up from the pillowcase

wafting over me like your fuck fever

is her drugstore floral passion toilet water

sour from her last night's quickie with you

stomach fluids mix too familiar in my mouth

your mustache is a cactus I cannot unfeel

after your play

you tell me to leave

to run! run!

she will be home any second

so I do

but I can't feel my legs

instead I hover home

a ghost

back across the street, wingless

get the mail, nothing for me

a want ad for my long gone dad

in my room, knees bent close

journal in hand, I pick up the fastest pen

pause for a long long time then

ink kisses paper chaste on the cheek

but I don't remember the end

ABUSER ERASURE[+]

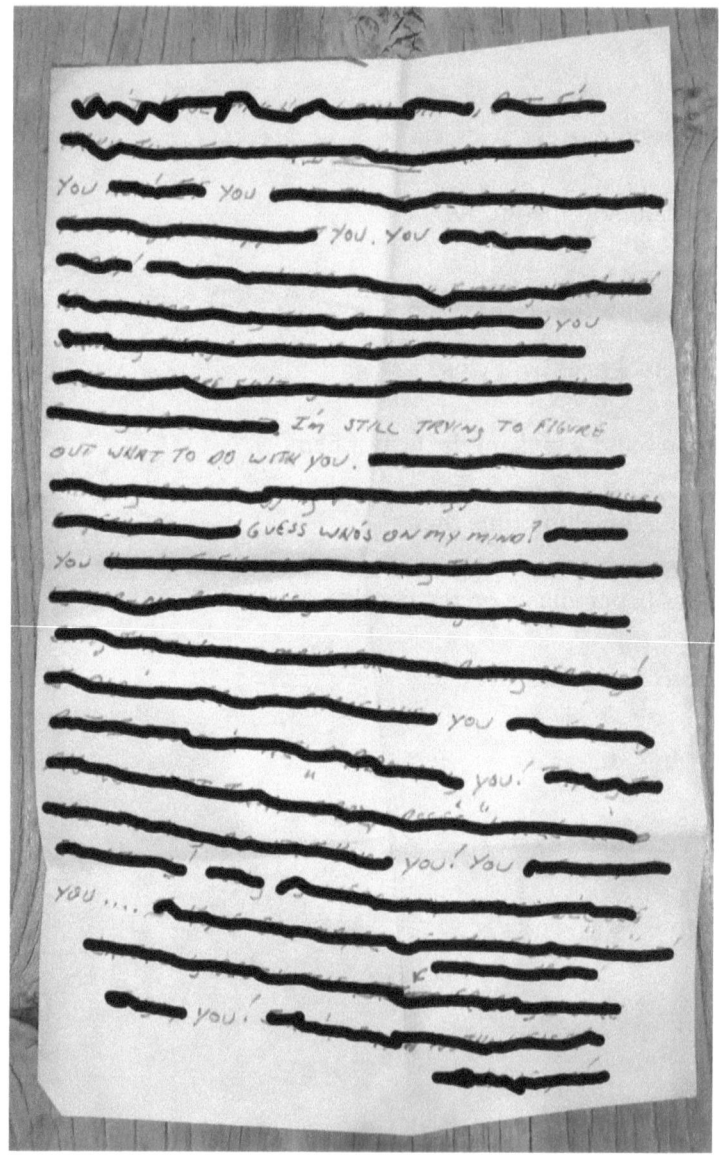

YOUR EYES

look straight ahead
to invite me closer

orbs of open book
infinity
a chocolate sea
occasionally blue
even more rare
one of each

wisdom languaged
in horse sign
teach me the ways
of attention
attuning
tending and time

half shut and look away
ask me to slow down
or to wait

blinking eyes are yeses
and how you beckon me
near

lids close
when you are content
and the sonar you send

off your lashes

is the bowline that moors
my heart

LIVING ROOM PICNIC

no fried chicken or sandwiches

no pickles or deviled eggs

no fizzy water

no pie

no brightly patterned blanket to lie on

no fresh air or puffy white clouds

to play games in or under

only the smell of dishes

waiting since yesterday's breakfast

the microwaved dinner the night before

burned coffee spilled on the counter

jellied egg on the floor

having missed the trash can

dingy light pries through smeared windows

the sound of shh's to the three small children

worming and whining across her lap

hoping to wedge themselves

between their fresh born sister

at their mother's milk-full breast

her free arm holding multiple tiny shoulders

we sit in an off kilter triangle

on bare linoleum floor

me slightly edged closer to him

she tries to pull her tattered

skirt down across her calves

soft and unshaven

the length of my 17 year old legs

on full display

his wide hand reaches over

to claim my naked knee

my chest puffs a bit

lifts

my chin tilts up at an angle

we hear him say that we will

like each other

take turns with him

how getting to know each other

would be prudent

that we ought to go on a date

I meet his wife's heavy blues

ringed and smeared in tear smudged

too heavy too many days old mascara

my unpainted browns cut

into her

hers cut back

I shrink

lean away look down

tug the hem of my shorts

there's not much to pull

one of the little boys

moves mewling toward his father

he's brushed off roughly

an unwanted speck of dirt

he goes down hard on his rump

the small mouth opens

to sniffle his protest

I automatically reach out

to touch his small blond head

the man rises

standing over us he reigns

offers to take care of the kids

and right then

we are sent out

together

he pulls the crying infant

from her straining arms

advises

we go to dairy queen

share a blizzard

and we do

HAWK+

1.

it took me a long time
to go to sleep
last night
the hawk
so high in the top
of the tree
riding the sky
calling me out
and pointing
screaming *you you*

I turn over
change my pillow
to the cool side
I don't want to hear him

I give you medicine

2.

I caught him
in my hands
on the ground
wings out
in the middle
of my fresh hatched flock
my chicken hatchlings
little pretend children

without a thought
how he could hurt me
I raced to him
with my arms open

clasped his wings and tucked them closed

my neck is sweaty
sticking me
to the silk membrane
of my pillowcase
I pull my knees up
throw my arm
across my ear and temple

3.

I scooped him up
chick children scattering
safe

silent and huge
between my hands
I held him to my chest
breathed in the wild air
coming off his feathers

forgot anything
in that moment
but wanting
that wild
to keep that wild
down inside of me
safe

4.

in my hands at 13
my father freshly gone
and here
I discover his attention
tethered to me

I am his as he is mine
we are starbound

5.

I throw off the covers
count my inhales
count my exhales
I knew I had to let him go
wanted to let him go
needed to let him go
his bright eyes
fluttering heart told me
it was right

I hesitate a moment
I wanted to go with him
to keep seeing him
soaring
in the sun
even when I can't sleep
pushing my legs straight again
my palm smooths
the sheets
your feathers float
across my closed eyes

6.

I admired you for a long time
told you things
thanked you
carried you to the corner
sat you high
up on that fence post
opened my fingers
squatted quickly down
and looked up at you

I waited
you waited

ruffled and fluffed your feathers
one floated down
you picked up one foot
and scratched your cheek
turned your head
found my eyes

I give you medicine

our lifetimes interchange

merge
morph
you blinked slow
turned your head back
opened your wings

and lifted

you flew high and away
I watched you
until you were gone

my heart soaring
with wanting
to companion you

feather in my hand

7.

on my back
I pull my covers to my chin
I imagine and remember
you flying away
lifting
soaring
seeing
I hear you scream

I give you medicine

softening into the sheets
I let the dark
lift me
let sleep take me
I slip in between
this day and tomorrow
and in my dream

I am you

A DIFFERENT STORY

the first hour after
I told myself it hadn't happened

struck dumb, then mute
folding inward, mind closing down

to the shower, witness of ablutions
unusual and futile

to the page for the purging
a different story pouring out

making it up as I go
the new words making it so

it didn't happen that way
this couldn't be true

it was *this* way
I swear to myself

there was a real bed and it was soft
I said yes and he was gentle

pencil moving erratically
crossing all the lines

hearing mom downstairs, making dinner
fried potatoes, onions with cheese
I sit down crookedly
I smile

translucent and clammy
looking like dinner itself

QUEEN

even though I'd switched
off all the lights
and made it cave dark
in my room
I still crouched
cringing
under the windowsill

knuckles the color
of my nightgown
there was no way you could see me

I'd told you
so boldly bravely
I didn't want
to ride around this week
how big-girl of me
I'd stopped taking
your calls

so you started coming
around at night
always at night
felt like every night

I peer
over my fingertips
listening
the music growing
louder slowly

my clue you were close
again
my cue to hide
deeper
into my darkness
your neon yellow four door
chevy
impala so fast
would go so slow
you crept you creep
you crawl by
back and forth
your tires crunch the dark
munch the gravel black top

your windows rolled
all the way down
mine only barely cracked
enough to hear
the show must go on
over and over
you'd play it
you used to say it
the show must go on
over and over
and over

you slowly drive by
I see your naked arm
first bent at the elbow
then extend to straighten
the fist opens and turns palm down
it rides the gentle night air
as if you were still touching me

sometimes you would stop
on the street

music still roaring loud
even with my window dark
second story street side
you knew right where to look
I'd fall and flatten myself
to the floor
nightgown grown damp
with the stamp of fear

will you dare
come to the door
again
will they let you in
again

the strain of listening
for movement
the slam of a door
collapses my chest
in a punch

you'd roll on
same song blaring
I never wondered
what the neighbors thought
or if they knew

faint notes of queen
no longer rule me
I know you're gone
even so
I'd go get
into the closet
close the door
just in case

startling awake

aching and cramped
I'd listen for long
minutes
and minutes more
then crawl into bed
pray to no god that
tomorrow be different

DYAD

_____ Night _____

his heat wave

will not warm nor soften

my stiff body

a frozen dinner

laid on the bed

he reaches for his fork

beneath the belt

eight course terror

snakes up from below

my waist

scars roots clog my throat

closed

_____ Day _____

I chance to dare

a daydream come

the wished-for-caress

a silk fuzz muzzle kiss

to nibble the breeze

across my cheek

and for my spine

to ribbon out

across your back

tall and sweeping

ample and broad

my curly chocolate crown

to brush the bushy

dock of your tail

my arms hang down

open like jesus

to cradle your barrel

I scan sky castles

passing above

as you graze greens

the clover

below

HERD MEDICINE

Dear Misty,

Not long after we transplanted to Texas, I was introduced to a POA. You were a Pony of the Americas and came to live with me at the one-story yellow house when I turned eleven. I arranged my room so the headboard of my bed rested even with the windowsill. I kept the screen for that window under my bed. You could reach your neck all the way into my room, the next best thing to living in the barn, which my mom would not let me do. People might have thought you hung out through the window only for the daily carrots. Which of course you did get. But we knew it was more than that. How many times did I wake from an afternoon nap with your lip drooping on the pillow next to me? In relationship with you, I began to sense the meaning of friendship that transcended words.

Friends exchange gifts and share activities. We certainly attended many play days, gymkhanas, endurance rides, beach trips, and swims and even experienced a runaway or two. To stay in shape for my middle school track meets, with you on a halter and lead line, I would run beside you as you would seem to fly in a spectacular extended trot next to me. Time after time, you taught me even more powerful than the doing-ness of things is the being-ness of things.

We didn't give you a choice with the horse shows, parades, and trailer rides to the beach. But you did make the choice to do with me what even some of the best of friends cannot do. Hang together in silence. I'd journal or nap and there you'd be, nearby, often with your long jawbone slung over my shoulder. As if to keep tabs on my well-being through my written words or the content of my dreams.

Those were the early years of growing pains. My beloved blue-and-white trucker cap said "Love to Ride," and I'd have pulled it down to the bridge of my nose if I could have seen well enough to ride. Our move to South Texas was an about-face culture change. A place where asking questions in class got me in trouble almost as much as when I'd forget to say ma'am after yes or no.

After school I would ride you bareback several miles each way to the ball field for practice. Softball wasn't available, so girls had to play baseball. Very few did. My position was catcher. I became the first girl to ever hit a home run in my town's Little League history. I still have that baseball.

Misty, you hardy mare, you bore my blooming confusion with a back like a duck. You remained unvexed by my assertive attitudinal exploratory blunders. The suffocation I experienced in school I began to answer with pushback at home and onto you. Soon, when any bossy challenge I presented began to go too far, you'd stomp my foot with your hoof, whap me good with your tail, refuse the jump or even to move at all. You remained stalwart and sure until I righted myself and my attitude.

Later, in apology, I'd again offer the carrot through the window, crack my journal in an attempt to self-decode, and when you could have walked away, Misty, your eyes once again would gently blink and close, and after a long whuffling sigh, with my pencil running away across the page, your speckled lips would sink deep into my pillow.

Thank you, sweet mare.

Love,

Christin

ABDICATION

I am barely breathing

my chest doesn't move at all

my diaphragm jammed tight

at half mast

you don't notice

your rough and worn cattleman's hands

busy pulling

me closer

into the length of your soft

pancake and pork pie bellied body

your red bristly beard scratching

a bramble against my thin cold nape

my knees squeeze shut

my eyes lock out the light

and I've lost track

of your hands

my mind turns down

between the covers of my mother's

bed

we share now

I drown

what the hell?!

my attention snaps open

at her voice ripping

into the ugly moment

turning I see over his shoulder

her standing there

hands empty and open

mouth hanging down

eyes popping past

their picture frame bones

her stare smothers

his ludicrous fire

and evacuates the air

from the room

from my already dry land lungs

in slow motion her hand

lifts to the door knob

her face a slow-blur whip around

she turns her back to me

closes the door

leaving me there

alone

taking my life with her

HIS ARMS

command my attention
fat meaty bats
coming my way
block the door

broad web of hands
weave fear through the loom
of his fingers

forearms filleted open
like fish on the sand
red running to the sea
and onto the floor

his hands on places
that close my throat

CUTTER[+]

I open the door

the smell

cloying

sticks its fingers too deep in my nose

I can't even see for a moment

my heart gallops away, bit in its teeth

ice water drains down my spine

chilling my skin, wetting my clothes

my palms weep

in an instant I step in and see

bed askew and turned

the dark and growing pool on the floor

two arms hanging down

looking unattached

unwanted anymore

familiar forearms, heavy as hams

shredded crossways over and over

over and over

unbelievably I imagine a wide ribbon

I could weave over and under

and through

over and under and through

your meat I could sew

back together into something pretty

fear fingers down into my throat

gagging me

daring me to run, needing me to

the once-shiny blade

now wet and fresh painted

hides under the bed

my body and mind recoil away

disappear as I am standing there

colliding back into the room

a flashbang

I leap across the pool

like hanuman

scoop your runny arms up like

bread loaves

your body weighs 1000 pounds

I carry you like a baby

to the bathtub

later once they take you away

to the psychiatric rehab

an inhale arrests me

it looks like a slaughterhouse

someone has to clean it up

I am already too late for class

so alone

I do

MANE

your hands seem to go to it
gravitate magnetize
you want to touch it
tangle into it
brush it with your fingers
braid it unbraid it

emerging from the center line
it stands straight up
when first coming out
then folds to one side gradually
when volume exceeds verticality
it can be shaken from left to right
settling in between itself
until its lay pattern does assert
no pesky comb can triumph

you turn your hand up
losing sight of your skin
underneath its weight
fingertips find the origin
the crest of the neck
the top of the wave
you tickle the feathery furry place
draw your palm forward
to bring the sea of it
close to your face
you inhale and never want to exhale
the smell reminding you of somewhere
mane took you before

your heart wanting the ticket to return
an ocean in reunion
with the shore

fist both hands
wind it gently around your wrists
as many times as you can
as if you could hold onto yourself
to time going by
to slow it down if not reverse it

to me the heavier the better
you could crawl into it
retreat a while
unwrap your wrists
you cannot stay but welcomed
to return often
the single hair that's stuck
in your fingernail
you can keep
use it to mark this time travel
a time capsule of no time passed
you get acknowledged with permission to touch
that sigh you heard when you stepped
close to the hooves

hot cumin ground nutmeg
between-the-toes-cinnamon
mixed with the fuzz
you can scrape off the sycamore leaf
funnel it into your nostrils
smelling yourself high
it turns you back by the shoulders
to what's current in your world
to match your upturned lips
and fresh lifted cheeks

but now
with your chin tilted
to the sky

UNAWARE

of lightning striking my body from inside every cell

I walk around with singed hair and burnt out eyes

toes blown off my feet

at the dining table

at my desk in english class

in the locker room changing for volleyball

in the grocery store choosing unbruised apples

picking up horse feed

shopping for shoes the next size up

legs with chopped off ankles

carrying secrets I still don't know I have

this all well before the doctor notifies my mother

she has fragmentation of the self

I leave evidence and clues

tiny embers

char

still warm

they swept them away as part of their day

a chore

so subtle and complete the evisceration

no one even notices

the balding girl with peeling crispy skin

and no feet

I cannot run

I am unaware of myself and so are they

until they get close and smell

and feel the furtive-caged-in-tightness

we all choke on a small cough

and don't know why

we casually move on

doing homework

caring for the chickens

washing dishes after dinner

skin sloughing off even as mom

looks at me and asks about my day

neither of us notices

but both move to clean up the small crumblies

I've left behind when I shift away

from the sink

what is that

I hear myself ask

oh probably something you tracked in from the barn

you say

go on and get ready for bed I'll finish up here

in sudden electrocution I am lit up from the inside

blinding

I can't even move

then comes another crack of thunder that roars

my insides out

and I don't feel the shearing

knifing me from my heart through my forearm

this time

my bubble pink tee shirt darkening to black

maroon penny red showing where my

heart might be

I amble on through the living room

brothers watching tv

hey

hey

my hands moving to my face as I climb

the first step

ozone in my nose

what is wrong with me

back against the door and I close myself in

the only thing I can do is to

rewrite the ending again

for the millionth time

this time what he did

instead

when my baseball bounced into his yard

was pick it up without the pause

smile

say *here you go kiddo*

and throw it back across the street

like a healthy married man with small children

would do

I write

"my glove reaches up to catch it

and I do"

AFTER YOU LEFT[+]

what happened to you
what happened to you
that you could walk into a room
and see me sitting there
with him
naked to my waist
and walk out

over the back of the couch
armpit high
you could see my breasts
with his hands on them
and his eyes feeding there

what happened to you
did it happen to you too
when you were my age
or earlier or later
who did it
what did they do
did anyone know

you walked out on me
leaving his hands
where you found them
the look on your face

was it in your room your house
in a car
did someone scare you

into a corner

how did you learn to stay quiet
you taught that to me
who taught it to you
did they tear your clothes
or bruise you
tell you not to tell or else
I learned my breasts were bad
they were ugly
and needed to be covered
the shape of your face said so
after you left
I cried
his hands stayed where they were
kneading stroking
massaging my tears into them
with his hard devilcruel mouth

I wanted to go with you
but you left without me
slamming the door
who did it to you
did they look like him
who stole your power
who stole your voice
what allowed you to swallow
instead of speak
what propelled your legs to move away
rather than strongly stand

what are you afraid of
it's been so long and my breasts
aren't that shape anymore
no longer that firm and high
that couch is gone
he is gone

but I still feel
him on me
and you still
walk away

leaving me behind stuck in the nest
unable to fly
who gave you the scissors
you used to clip my wings
keeping me stalled keeping me silent

what happened to you
that disempowered you so completely
that you'd rather offer me your shame
than the power of your voice

12 STEPS

it used to be
tornadoes of creature-screaming
cruel smack of leather
against drenched skin
dust obscuring eyes
no breath no mercy
human whooping
zzzzz of rope
snubbing pole too tight
hooting hollering slapping hee hawing
groaning straining bursting-body-down
two legs conquering four

but now the
pasture is the size of an ikea parking lot
she whistles from the gate
halter and leadline hang loosely
from bent elbow
in plain view

out of his snooze ears perk
head lifts neck turns
he looks
a ripple flows across his velvet bay skin
1230 delighted pounds
turning her way

whinnying loud
his magnetized moon body
ambling arrowed

straight to her earth
into a trot he
breaks all barriers

her skin glory rippling
seeing him
his eyes smiling in silent approach
wide white starred forehead
landing smack gently dab
into the center of her chest
embracing without arms

on the mounting block a saddle
a bridle-with-no-bit
hoof pick a soft brush
not a carrot to be found
she speaks to him
telling him this pointing out that

with a two fingered whisper touch
to his crown
she asks him to lower his head
gently down
bridle layered over his ears
one at a time
she smooths his forelock

inviting his attention
to the saddle pad slow
then the leather lowers
onto his back
he yawns and melts his eyes closed

he's moved near the gate
thinking they'll go out
he turns to look at her and ask

aren't we
with my voice I say

"I am over here
if you'd like me to get on
you will need to turn around and
come back"

a lifetime to cross
nothing but mercy
no breath and a beat
skips
two
three

then with a muffled sigh and a lick and chew
he turns and doesn't stop walking
closing 12 steps of separation
until he's aligned his saddle with
the teardrops on her toeboots
she slides onto his back
her soul replaced

four legs conquering two

GRANDSTAND[+]

too thin ribs of
aluminum stadium seating
bore in
grinding trench lines
up and down my back

the words no
and stop
and no
no
no
clog my throat
and cut off my air

my ability to hear
see
know
feel
drifts up and away
like smoke circling a magic trick

except this is too real

time stands nearby
stopped
and helplessly watches

beams of light slice through
the apparition of my split body
floating out across the football field

am I the hiked ball sailing
across the goalpost
the faraway grinding seems to stop
rough arms pull me up
off the bleachers
I am dragged down the stands
through the stadium
toward the exit
without knowing how
I pull up my pants

his arm comes across my shoulders
somehow my legs swing like walking
but my shoes don't touch the ground

meeting the flashlight with eyes that cannot focus
past their pinholes
my brain seizes
my backbone raw
I try to grasp and place
like a game of memory
the black and white car
and what could be projecting
that piercing light

perhaps I am dead and
going through the tunnel

"everything alright here?"

punches me in the gut
with the dawning
it's a policeman

the arm across my shoulders
bends at the elbow
his fingers handcuff

the back of my neck
signal me silent
we stop too far away
the law can't see
my two wide foxholed eyes

"oh yeah all good just talking nice night huh"

the officer stops moving toward us
swings his light back and forth
between his face and mine

"alright then well y'all move along and make your way out of here now"

"yessir we will now just need to grab something I left in the stands"

"have a good night"

"thank you sir"

I don't feel the tears sliding out
as I watch the black and white car
back up and drive away

his fingers grip hard now
I'm turned back around
marched back the way we'd come
back up to the ramp
back into the stands

"we gonna finish what I started"

a wet blanket strapped down
over my face
couldn't have suffocated me more
than those words
they seemed to fall out of his mouth

through the air to the ground without making a sound
I never heard him say them
but so many many too many years later
my bones still repeat them

all at once like a magic trick
cloaked in smoke
and white doves
I am back
standing by my car
alone
not knowing how my feet walked me here
favorite barrette lost from my hair
jeans half zipped
blouse ripped
but my shoelaces are still tied

"you better go home"

he yells across to me from his car
where he's climbing in
I turn my head toward him
my eyes can't meet his
land instead on his keys
flashing in his fist

"and wash yourself out with coke"

he slams his door
starts the car
puts it in gear
I watch him drive away
little pieces of gravel spurt out
from under his tires
a puff of fumes
left in his wake

I am still mute
standing there alone
wondering
how exactly
and why
to put coke in my vagina

but somehow later

I do

HERD MEDICINE

Dear Bobby,

High school years found me astride you, Copy Leo, now having graduated from pony owner to the big world of full-size horses. You were jet black in winter, with a single white star on your forehead and a thick black mane and tail. I called you Bobby for short. *Phar Lap* was my favorite movie now, the underdog story of a chestnut Australian racehorse who became a national hero, and he was nicknamed Bobby. It fit you. We were inseparable.

You stretched me and my horse-training skills wide, especially since you were just a three-year-old when I bought you. And with my own money too.

These tumultuous years found me painfully discovering my second set of wings. The first wings of childhood unveiled themselves so easily. This teenage set, still dark with wet stickiness and stubbornly stuck, plastered to my shoulder blades, kept me tucked in on myself and uncertain. The times I felt confident enough to fly were always up high on your back. When I stood on my own two feet, I felt unwieldy and ineffective. The ground felt unfamiliar and scary. But riding the mountain of your back above your four hooves gave me the view from heaven and hawks' eyes. It was here I could find my own globe.

There were more beach trips with ecstatic screams of freedom, galloping down long, shiny hard-packed stretches where sand meets ocean. The blisteringly fast rhythm of your flashing hooves hollowed out the earth, leaving stars in the wake behind us.

Still more times of being out of control, where, Bobby, you would take the bit between your teeth to fly on your own. You challenged me to decide between hanging on or doing some solo flying of my own by jumping off! Those times of leaping off versus clinging on taught me equally. The ability to ride a runaway or launch off what felt like a bullet train showed me that no matter what choice I made, I would always find my way back to myself through the body of a horse.

We joined the mounted drill team and competed locally and statewide. You and I became co-leaders, then went on to become leaders together. The emotional teenage turmoil of these years was punctuated by the piercing of my whistle. Each of our intricate routines, five or six songs long, would be performed at a canter and sometimes a full-out gallop. Human and horse, each blowing hard by the end with breathlessness and exhilaration. You knew the maneuvers even better than I, anticipating every change of direction with surgical precision. At one of these competitions at the height of your glory, I was approached by a well-known horseman in the area and offered a blank check for you. He shook his head and smiled as I refused. My flowering ability to lead was born from this time on your back, my wings beginning to unfold. Consensual leadership seeds dropped into my earth every time I rode you.

There was no discussion regarding my senior pictures. We did them together.

During my first year of college, it seemed we both began to lose our footing simultaneously. I began to slip away, lost to the clutches of undiagnosed PTSD, while you developed a hoof disease called navicular and had to retire. You gave me the courage to move beyond you, and those earlier planted seeds of resilience began to sprout.

The senior-year photos of you and me still hang in my mother's hallway.

Thank you.

Love,

Christin

WHILE CASTRATING BULL CALVES[+]

despite the twisted tunnel traveled
I'm still a tender hearted twenty
away at school
homesick for my horse
through a country contact
in exchange for board
I found a ranch nearby to work

invisible to myself by now
the foreman takes my measure
and when he licks his lips
assesses me a heifer
that I would come to push
through a maze to nowhere
and check her legs
peer behind her tail
to check for things in place

I am knuckled blind
by history's vulgar familiarity
the gesture slips right by
that he's seen me slabbed
buck naked
across some fathomed
dinner plate

the heat hard days
callous both my hands and me
the hours he requests
engorge themselves to years

slack tired by the break for lunch
I climb into the truck
made to sit the middle seat
in front
a man on either side
the shifter racked between my legs
second gear his favorite grind

and later only vaguely
does it register rancid
bile that rises as the cowboys
take their beer and leave
he gives me one more chore to do
and then another

so after when he roughly
bends me rubber boned without resist
over toyota tailgate
dirty long day jeans
bunched about my ankles
my knees poked out for his ingress
I turn my head so it won't bang
and feel nothing at the sight
of daisies and bluebonnets
carpeting the fields
the distant deer munching on
in their contentment

I force my laugh to resist my cry
at his recount of stories borne of hell
to scare one day his best friend
he emptied out fried chicken
and in its place he coiled
in the greasy bottom
of the bucket
a rattlesnake whose mouth

he sewed closed with wire
and when that friend nearly fainted
in his fright
my foreman chortled gaily
then sliced the rattle for a prize
tossed the tragic creature swirling
into the ditch to die
immuring my own shiver flesh
I hide my teeth
but make my lips turn up
for him to register a smile

in spring sorting
he shoves a pair of bloody cutters
in my hand
the bawling calf
locked tight
in squeeze chutes iron jaws
he showed me what to do

the tail is taken in reverse
over bovine spine
pressed down and despite the scream
you push

shit pours out but you can't care
you grab the skin below the balls
a handful with the knobs
above your fist

with these dirty cutters
you scissor
off a line of felted skin
and pitch it to the dogs

reach up inside the cavity
it's warm

you yank the bloody balls
slice away the veins and vesicles
just anything attaching
don't worry about the screaming

add them to the bucket
swum deep with slime
and cream white eggs
guarded by the dogs

now you do it

the next white eyed calf
slammed tight and set and squalling
I stare transfixed
hesitate too long
I learn his boots of crocodile
and how the ends are shaped
they come to points
hard into my ass
not once but twice
and many more

you hear the others laugh
gloved hands slapping their shoulders
I wipe the mix of ooze and tears
off my cheeks to see

and like the prisoner
who has no chain
I take the weapon
in the hand
that is not mine
and inflict as I am taught

horror
just the same

WHITE

nightgown at seven

      dawn fog veil   frothing free   behind her
small hands   curl in mane   galloping bareback   laughter
                                reins

cotton eyelet panties at seventeen

        man fingers   force past lace   parting lips
her head turns   to stare   out the window   blind   into dark

wedding dress at thirty-seven

    twice now   been walked   down the aisle   close danced
        happy tears toasts   ate cake   then laid down

feeling nothing

HYPERVIGILANCE

three people
second story
one window
a single tree lonely grey
peers through the grimy glass at me

the box-cramped room with its too warm air
stale and still
starts to close in
as we begin
our hour of fifty minute therapy

I see a white board wedged
between knees and floor
her hands splay fake
lavender pale nails
red and blue dry erase
markers lace her
right hand fingers
looped through
like a playground game

I sweat

she points to the board
and taps
her mouth moves
she must be speaking
words I cannot hear
a buzz sounds suddenly

slicing shocks and trips me
an electric fence it rips me
open my ears burn
my spine whips
stock straight
I scan her face
his face
it's clear they have no recognition
they haven't heard
what I
have heard

my hands sweat
on the couch beside me
pushing down
to be ready
to push me up

is that an alarm!
do we need to evacuate
the building

two blank faces
stare at me
interrupt my flighting
upward rising

oh sorry, that's my phone alarm
from yesterday she says
reminding me to call and check
on my daughter

the next seconds last
two days
he looks at me sideways
then straight ahead at her
their mouths move

another silent movie
my nerves still shiver
I sink to sit and sweat
our time is up
it's ten till noon on friday
five minutes from our house
I am still alone
and do not know why
or the way
home

CELIBATE

I did not agree to kneel
and make this vow
as brahmacharini
to emerge adorned
in robes of icicle fringe

never dripping salty honey
never to wear the bee's perfume
never to tickle intimacy's toe

my own trembling berry
in welcome never peeled
my glacial rose unbloomed

husband is right here
resting next to me unreal
calm gentle eternal and rare
safe steady and slow

but diamond rings
don't come with bandaids
no matter the size of wound
or carat

though into daily forward fold
of prayer this body beloved I bow
as lifelong self-sworn yogini
chastity is not my desire's due

breathe baby
baby breathe
your lips are turning blue

BAD THERAPY[+]

not used to driving in traffic
I scan wildly for the exit
fists slick grip the wheel
wishing now I hadn't decided to do this
no one in the passenger seat
to help with the map
she wouldn't have held my hand
but the map yes

spotting it I careen across three lanes
horns squealing at my thoughtless rush to the right
holding myself close to the wheel
waiting for red to turn green
I turn left drive straight turn right turn right
park
I don't lock the doors there's nothing to steal

my clothes announce what state I'm in
three damp pastures expanding into dry land
inside the lobby the chill bites me
I find her floor
the elevator comes and I push buttons

I get out
I don't register my legs moving
my hips sitting

suddenly I am before her
come in

the unseen movie screen
in her office
empty and blank
humming in wait
my story still gridlocked
inside me

after flimsy flappy chitchat
she asks from behind her desk
and her piles of papers
what brings you here?

I stumble out how I'm trying to get help
I'm hurting
not functioning
staying stuck in my room
maybe someone hurt me
home from university after they found me
locked in the bathroom

a hailstorm crashes out
each story stone snaps a wire
in the fence
propping up my heart

the screen begins to glow
like it's waking from sleep

we must've got to the part where
I'm alone in the room with him

where are you?
                      a boardinghouse for men.
were you alone?
                      yes. no I was with him, he was there.

how did you get there?
                         my mom let me borrow the car.
what time of day?
                         it was dark outside.
what were you doing?
                         I don't know. lying there.

the movie began to play inside my mind
no popcorn or milk duds for this horror show
how is this playing
where did she get this
from the last one
I wonder if they share stories
were all clients' movies shared this way
I am distracted by my own questions
as she's pointing to my imaginary screen

see there, look you are smiling
I look

all I see is a virginal girl grimacing
in front of a grown man
his hands
on her shoulders
pushing her down

on the bed
his meaty forearms cross her body
the screen flickers in and out
closing in from all sides
the content too wrong to play

then I hear her say
surely some part of you wanted it
was even enjoying it

what
the
fuck

again she says
you were there you must have been enjoying it
you must've asked for it

it

the screen playing the part
where he pushed his fingers
roughly through white panties
the girl's arms bent
palms up
surrender
playing dead

I am watching it replay and flash back
again and again on the broadcast
behind my eyes

I don't hear her anymore
the room has long since gone away
it's only me watching the screen
play and play and play and play

you must've wanted it
the only thing I can hear

the light gets sucked
into the vacuum in my head
I fall away
splinter into dark

I am back in my car
the hands on the wheel
unrecognizable

nothing was stolen

I WARNED YOU

to reassign myself alone / toward home / swimming back through the light / **studded black velvet** / untouched / to never be held / inside what's left of your **heart** / like shrapnel / by a piece of longing / with a penta-shaped **scar** / you'll forever be marked / and it has / once your fist closes / marriage / before the inevitable terrible / last attempts to detract you / to distract you / tossing shards of shine this way and that / bitter I was / out of your world / chased me into the blackness / thinking to catch this glittering bride / you pursued me anyway / my warning spell uncast / away / then fading / bright and boldly / shimmering and shooting / I said no and sidestepped / I did / I warned you / like now / I'll hurt you / no / and wear to your pleasing / **a jewel to reshape** / a gem to possess / I'm not what you thought / at this twist / disbelief / it's on your face / or release / I don't budge / trying to get me off / you shake me and shake me / until your eyes take me in / the shock of it won't register / mine too / yours and awfully / **blood** will run slippery without **reins** / the color of crimes uncaught / a wedge / tight / I'll stay lodged there / phalanges into bone / slice / then you will feel the cleaving pinch / because it will take two of them to hold me / both the left and the right / of your fist / through the creases / irretrievable / ragged hole punched / blackness will squeeze out first / to your surprise / here we go / I told you / your fingers close around me / I resign / you always do / I know / but you will / every surface a razor / **untouchable** / I am sharp sided / don't / I'm warning you / you will want to reach for me / sparkling too high / unreachable / I **shine**

BEFORE SLEEP COMES TO TAKE ME

even after all of this time
I cry a little bit

each night I uncurl
into sheets and blankets
that smell safe and feel like me
I cry a little bit

even if it's been a good day
with no memories on my skin
full of sun spring and birds

speaking their stories
clients singing and showing their pain
pointing to this place or that place
"it happened here"
"this part broke"
"I am empty"
"there is nothing left"

even when they leave smiling
more whole after especially good sessions
more given back to themselves
more unfrozen
more alive
more self-understood and safe
I cry a little bit

even if the softness and curve of the pillow
feel just right

the heaviness of the bedclothes
comforting this time
I cry a little bit

the places of zero
the carved out points
of my heart

eaten away worn down
ages ago
the time I've lost life I've lost
nights days smiles laughs moments
touch I couldn't feel
I've lost
so
much
time
I cry a little bit

no matter that I survived
appear whole
on the outside
the world sees me successful
bright
intelligent capable responsible reasonable

but there are years
gone
floated away

I cry a little bit

I eat grief every day
gorging even

yet I starve

I cry a little bit
each night
before sleep slides in beside me

IN MY HAIR

                cast out

    the noose snags

                    without bread or fare

  on the moons

                      set adrift without a sail

    snarls

                full moons ago

  for my soul

                  when it was lost

I am a stranger

              to myself

when for so long

                my me has lost its letter 'i'

inside and out

                                        looking into curling faces

                spent combing

                                        puzzling tarot in tea leaves

                dumped in trash

                                        under midnight lamps

        over the neighbors'

                                new high fence

searching for the last little "i"

                                        dug up roots of limbs

                tree and skin

                                        wrapped in earthworms

                spent hunting

                                        falling into sandy slumber

        cloudy thundersky motif

                                I sniff and turn

        a riding figure emerges

                                        caressing brunette waves

        taps my shaking shoulder

my lovely lonely i-treasure

only in yourself

I am found

HERD MEDICINE

Dear Smoke,

I can't even remember how I came to have you. You were like an apparition and simply appeared in my world. You bore resemblance to your name with your long charcoal mane and tail and your glossy fine coat, the color of multiple shades of ethereal grey. You glimmered in the night, and your ghostliness seemed to make you disappear in the light of day. You became a night shepherd.

At this time of my life, I was several years into college as a philosophy major because majoring in horses wasn't an option. But every weekend I would drive three hours each way to come home to be with you. I had since lost myself completely with no map and no access to the compass of my heart.

Only later did I recognize how you had become the safety net I desperately needed at that time. You were strong and powerful in stature, gentle and charismatic in nature. You became the rock, solid and stoic, that I thrashed my own helplessness upon every weekend. Unknowingly, I projected all my suppressed aggression and sorrow directly on you. I had long since stopped listening to anything inside or outside of me, including horses. Exactly as people had refused to listen to me, I enacted this same omission during our training sessions, when I would attempt to force your proud body into a particular carriage or frame, using homemade draw reins. These barbaric contraptions would mechanically leverage your head down to a more acceptable height and place according to me and my arbitrary specifications. You remained unbroken and kind.

Of course I had no idea of the cruel play I was reenacting on your majestic being. Smoke, your animal body absorbed my pain, yet your spirit refused my punishment in the graceful way only an enlightened one could do. You transcended me and yet remained present in life, to partner with me in my own imbalanced process to try to right myself. I have no doubt you must have made this sentient choice on behalf of me, in the place-no-place beings gather before they incarnate here.

I made the decision to sell you to raise the funds I needed for a short-term opportunity as a working student that would take me back to Maine to study with an Olympic medal–level dressage trainer. For a long time after letting you go, my heart felt like a tough piece of meat when a serrated knife makes a long, slow slice across it, only reaching halfway through.

To this day when I think of you, gorgeous horse, and the time we were together, my heart skips a beat in shame and regret. Then feathers of self-compassion and forgiveness always put a momentary catch in my breath. I will never cease to make amends, by sending silent prayers of gratitude to you and your not-of-this-world wisdom, and bids for your forgiveness. Thank you, gorgeous boy.

Love,

Christin

THE COLLIDING BODY

the brown rapids of her hair
catch your attention first
a grotto of fronds unfurling wild

the open highway of her neck
you could go wide open on
but for the scarves she wears
are blocking
this unmapped spot land-locking

you might want to trespass
but you wouldn't dream of it
collar bones create rivulets
veins criss cross the river delta
on the way down to the sea

first you must ford her
alluvial fan arch
two
before gunning it toward her shallow island
on course to her offshore ice
a cliff

where you may not divert
for the whirlpools of her eyes
and the forks of her fists
will drown you

if only it had been so

DOCTOR'S OFFICE

on the exam table

I wait

with the crispy white

paper

my hands

make prints by my hips

my thighs stick

I peel them

up

down

the paper tears

the door opens

no knock

GOOD THERAPY

the waiting room has plants
even real ones sometimes
gentle yellows remind of sunny kitchens
with fresh bread or chocolate chip cookies
coming out of the oven
to break open while still warm
the chairs invite you to sit all the way in
not just on the ledge
magazines are thoughtfully set out for you
even though you won't need to wait
overly long or much at all
windows are clean and actually look out somewhere green
a place for your breath to land
eyes to rest

she is welcoming
in the way your body believes
no convincing needed
sometimes she says
it's a beautiful day let's sit outside maybe walk
which is exactly what you were thinking
never dreaming it could be real
you are listened to
deeply with the whole body of her
far past the ears
a gentle invitation to show not just tell
point to the hurt places
say more about that
show me

it can come and go
as needed and without judgment
you are always welcomed back or supported to go
you are gently nudged and never pushed
one day she leads
next time you
the cha-cha forward and back
grapevine side to side

if you get lost she will look for you
leave breadcrumbs for you to find your way
back to your trail
not hers

there is intensity sincerity and
commitment to care
there is laughter and play
she might cry a few tears with you
offer permission to feel and be real
sharing the tissue box is ok

creativity and experiments are normal
ok I'll be here and you be there
and we start to walk
and let's see what happens
you might remember
at the point when we meet
intersecting parallels

there's drawing
collage
sand trays
toys and dolls
easels and markers
music and movement
and writing
she offers you sentences to finish

life is . . .
the thing I can't face is . . .
what I learned from my mother about life is . . .

she never scares you on purpose
she has lifelines to throw
if suddenly
you go under
then teaches them to you
so you can begin
to save yourself

it's kind honest and accountable
holds you responsible for your choices here on out
about the before she says
you did nothing to deserve it
you didn't ask for it
it wasn't your fault
with her the truths begin
finally to permeate
a tiny silver bell
ripples inside you

and if she's spooky good
she won't let you get away with poor me and pointing fingers
she will give you exactly what you need
without extra to wade through
shepherding you back away from the edge
toward yourself and what's true
what's gone past
what's now
and the power you retain
never actually lost
even after all that's happened to you
she lets you find it
all on your own
she doesn't hand it back like the missing sock mate

one day you finally begin to believe because
on a day you don't even see her
when you are fresh back from a predawn walk with the dog
the neighborhood and house still quiet
the coffee yet in your hand
the dew still wet on your feet
you catch a glimpse in the mirror
see a surprise
and you begin to believe

not in her

but in the smile glowing there
growing

WHAT ABUSE DOES TO YOUR MARRIAGE

you needed me
to hold you
at night
but your skin

stays untouched

you needed me
to reach for your hand
but it remains

an offering unanswered

you needed me
to find you
in my dreams
I remain

a no-show

you needed me
to wear the ring
but my fingers

are bare

you needed me
to tend the flowers
in the garden

but even the rosemary

is brown and wilted

you needed me
to be satisfied at home
the out-of-town property
searches printed in plain view

beside my chair

you needed me
to delight in my recipes
no drippy spoon rests and the pages clean
still pristine

the oven remains cold

you needed me
to fill our home corners with laughter
instead halls echo

crying with no sound

you needed me
to warm the sheets
scorch them on occasion
but they maintain their coolness

season round

you needed me
to include us
in my schedule
but the calendar is empty

you needed me

as fuel for flame
instead the hearth

is propane lit

you needed me
to long for you
instead of
space and sky

I just needed not to die

WHAT I COULDN'T SAY

1.

what I couldn't say was / you are too big for me / you are a man / I am a child

what I couldn't / say was / that I didn't know what the hell I was doing / there was no one around / to tell me what to do

what I couldn't say / was that I didn't want to go that night / out to that club / 45 minutes away / if I stayed / then he was at home / if I went / then I had to face you

what I couldn't / say was how desperate I was for attention / from anyone / I had no friends / I could tell / I was tough and angry / I scared people away / I still do

what I / couldn't say / was / that I was hungry so hungry / at lunch / watching all the kids eat / but if I eat I'll grow / and if I grow / I'll get bigger and / if I get bigger / I'll be visible / but I was anyway

what / I / couldn't / say / was how goddamn embarrassed I was / to have lunch at sixteen / with that man / our supposed-cousin / he was a pilot / I had no clothes washed / I didn't know what to wear / how to dress / I couldn't say / I don't want to go

2.

I'm afraid of you
Stop scaring me

Get your hand off my neck
Don't touch me
Help
I'm too young
This is not ok
No I don't want to do that
No
Stop
Get off me
It's not ok
Leave now
Don't come back
Get out of my room
No I don't want to take a ride
I'm not working for you anymore
Don't put your hands there
I am not fat
My spinal curve is perfect
I am beautiful
I am creative
My eyes are perfect as they are
Do not come closer
I'm calling for help
I'm not going with you
You are a grown man
I am a girl
Stay away from me
Get your hands off me
Protect me help me
I'm scared
I'm terrified
Who the fuck do you think you are
You need help
Get off my property
Get out of my house
Never come back
Never call here again

I need help
Someone is hurting me
Doesn't anyone care
It wasn't my fault
I don't want to go
Stop gripping my arm
You are hurting me
No
Don't do that
You scare me
I'm not coming with you
Don't touch me
No
Keep your hands off
You are not allowed near me
No no no no no no no no no no no
I feel alone
Who cares about me
Does anyone
Where are we going
Why are we stopping here
Get off me
I'm too young
Stay away
Get out
Leave now
I'm hurting
I want to live but maybe it's easier to die
No one will notice if I am gone
I need help
I'm confused
I don't know what to do
I'm scared
I'm embarrassed
I'm ashamed
I can't do this anymore

I want out
I'm afraid I'm dying
I'm dying
I was hurt
You did not protect me
You let me get hurt
You saw
You walked away
You left me
You invited them in
You were in on it
My jeans are too tight please notice
Tell me to change
Tell me I cannot go
Tell him to leave
Does anyone care
I am alone

3.

Help me
A man is hurting me
He is saying things that scare me
And putting his body next to mine
His eyes stare at my skin
His hard hands
Mold me in ways I don't understand
He makes shapes with my body that hurt
Stop
Don't
Just let me die

what else I couldn't say

that

I am saying

now

FUCK YOU MOTHERFUCKERS

HERE I AM AT 48

after a morning thirty-five lap swim
at the scuba swim pool down the street
after a call with a woman
wanting me to teach yoga at her
retreat
I end up counseling her in her business
on the house I say
then regret it
after scrambled eggs
with leftover asparagus
it begins to rain
after standing barefoot in the backyard
my face to the sky
teardrop touched
rare much-needed shower
the earth is parched
thirsty
after a short training session with lali
downward dog, sit, gimme five, down, rest, roll over
good treat!
after three hours playing copy editor
for my husband's new website
after after after
all
these
years
I am resting and reading your poems
reading poems about your mother
mother
dying

dying then dead then after
I realize now
right now
not
after
I am sobbing for the losing
my own
that will come
that I never had her

REALIZATION

it slapped me one sunday morning

I was about to take a sip
cup to lip
the fragrant warm curl
a genie snaking into my nose

the rim clicked my teeth
with its abrupt arrival
flash bulbing the message
across the inside expanse of my skull
familiar to knifing pain
of different truths

lowering my hands
I look up
gaze out the window
like I could see it
out there somewhere
past the bird feeder hung down from the oak arm
the chickadees congregating
chittering up a storm

past the long grasses of the back pasture
jockeying for first rays

past the fence outlining my property's shape
it might be floating out in the rice field
they flooded weeks ago
about to be pecked up

by the blue heron hunting for her breakfast
but no

it was in here
in the living room
sitting next to me on the pillow
I was about to drink it
again in the next sip
I was breathing it in
and had been

it was clinging
to my still warm-from-the-bed pajamas
it was prying my throat open
an sos tapping out on my tongue
the words shot out in one leap
a mantra
parting my lips
a hot-fired knife dipped in gall
the message snaps free
shattering my teeth

to break the spell you must tell.

ME (TOO)

I want you to taste

your own medicine

rancid toxin

and gag

I want you to feel

bloodworms

curdle the screams

in your throat

so no sound comes out

I want you to suffocate

with a handful of meat

wrapped around your neck

necktie tight

when you try to speak

or run

I want you to see

if you can swallow

after you look

into my eyes

and turn to stone

HERD MEDICINE

Dear Royal,

When I was in my early twenties, I was back at home after college, bedridden with depression. One day my mom came upstairs and sat on the edge of my bed. "I have an idea," she said. "What if we adopt a pair of mustangs? We'll each get one." Next thing I knew, we were in the truck on the way to a Bureau of Land Management mustang auction. It was the thought of you that got me out of that bed.

The early hours, days, and weeks we spent simply sharing space. You, vital and proud chestnut stallion, on one side of the fence, me on the other. I had to not only earn your trust for the sake of my own safety, but reciprocally illustrate my own worthiness of that faith. Which one comes first? Do I prove I am trustworthy and then you trust me, or do you believe in me and I prove I am trustworthy? I learned how the pixie dust of paradox opens the box of confidence to release a duo dance of vulnerability and bravery.

At first, you barely tolerated my presence. Then you came to allow it. The day you came to invite it was a day my heart exploded with belonging. Your head coming over the stall wall to sniff in greeting, then lick my outstretched hand in acceptance. I slowly reached my hand back to touch your neck and groom your withers with my fingers. We watered and nourished one another with respect and time. The seeds of our connection grew mighty.

With patience and reverence, as engaging in a sacrament, I brought you under saddle. Our first mounting as gentle as body surfing a slow rolling wave welcoming the shore into itself. We spent long easeful hours riding behind our house in the hundreds of acres of woods and fields. We rode the fence lines and followed deer paths. Sometimes forging new trails twisting between oaks and scrub and belly-high grass. We even jumped the occasional rice canal. We lost ourselves inside of time embedded with contentment and joy.

Your mustang self was a one-woman show. You rarely allowed others to pass across your boundary line. Royal, when it came time to geld you, I took the sedation injection out of my vet's hands, as they waited back at the fence line, and administered it to you myself while letting you know that all was well and I promised to make it up to you. I had been thinking about this for some time, how to manage taking you from stallion to gelding with honor and respect. Later that day, when you were back on your feet in the pasture grazing, claiming your recovery, I sliced cold butter into a skillet. Added minced garlic, shallot, and herbs. Once fragrant and bubbly, I tenderly lay prayers of gratitude and your fresh mustang oysters into the pan. You and your kin guided me through the crucible, to be initiated again, into the sacred centaur realm. I ate and was transformed.

Much too soon, we were confronted with an agonizing decision. Royal, you developed a monstrous abscess from multiple compacted teeth that began pushing your jaw out through your cheek. It was inoperable and had to be excruciating. You never showed that pain. I was told it likely stemmed from an early injury you sustained as a colt in the wild. I made a long braid in your mane and cut it. After our last goodbyes, we laid you gently down to eternal rest outside my bedroom window. That night I went to bed with a chestnut talisman in my hand and dreamed of you with ravens' wings instead of hooves.

Wild one, today your braid rides the rim of the brim of my favorite custom hat.

Love,

Christin

HEIGHT OF A HORSE IS MEASURED IN HANDS[+]

side by side
shoulder for shoulder
you languish above me
I am beneath you
below your high withers
so tall you are flying
our strides are
even and easy
attentive and gentle
hoof for foot we match
calm and the same
bound together in unspoken tether
our silent agreement
voiced
by soft lipped nibbles
and a velvety ear
tucked my way

you still there?

a horse language check-in
offered to me
I respond with a smiling sigh
and my heart slowing down
give you
my fingers curled softly
you bump touch lightly
to your mouth
your bay body the size of a ten by ten
eight hen chicken pen

concealing mine as we move
in steady reunion
under the bright innocence of the sun
on the road, two legs and forelegs
communion on ground
measuring hand over hand
you're a full 17
well able to hurt me
had you chosen to take lead
instead we walk, as friends
a companion of equals
seen in species not often
you so different than me
in the shape of our bodies
and numbers of forelimbs and hind
a horse and a girl
at pure liberty
no restraints from his way or mine
when we decide
on similarity

my spirit climbs
higher than the tower of your head
your neck swinging in time
to the cadence of innocents
walking each other down
the street toward relief
in wordless union
closing in on each other
the feeling of belonging
like the shape of your shoulder
staying with mine
choosing one another with respect
earned by trust without fists
each step a bandage
of healing and safety
transcribed in the sounds

of dual heartbeats and nickers
and clop clops of hooves

four eyes on the grass
on the side of the road
golding greens span along asphalt's edges
and you choosing again and again
with each step
to stay in the middle
with me
you not leading me
me not leading you
no distinction made between
no upper or lower
it's only us here, inside of our bubble
the world gone away
remaining in tandem
a true yes
a surrender to wounds
both in you and in me
coming closer to the home of healing
I've found your shadow and mine

A CHORALE OF SILENCE[+]

breaking silence   **silence breaking**

                     march

I sat you back down
at the table after dinner
saying how
we are going to have our own episode
of this is us
you looked scared
like some part of you knew
and dreaded that this moment
had now come

                                                        mom
oh my god what could this be
never seen her this serious
please don't let it be
oh my god it is

I thought I was smooth sailing
all set for my golden years

now what am I supposed to do

the only sound
my heart
not beating

brother

what I am about to say
won't be easy to hear
it will change the color of your
childhood
and I am so so sorry for that

what??
oh my god

I wish I had known
I would have done something

oh brother, thank you
you were a child
you couldn't have

but I would have done SOMETHING
I'm so so sorry

I remember he was always trying to get me to like him
he was scary

wait
if I was a child
then

so were you

we both were

mom
well maybe those experiences helped you
become the amazing woman you are today
look how many people you have helped

mom of all people you don't get to say that to me

brother

I am breaking the spell
that has bound me
for 35 years
I'm telling you this
so you won't rotely think
it can't happen to your family
protect your girls
protect my nieces

sorry that happened 'tin
maybe that's why you turned out so weird

geez I don't know what the fuck else to say
that shit'll never happen to my girls
I hope she leaves soon
this is too uncomfortable no idea what else to say
she's on her own
I'm out

you will overcome this setback

I laugh
instead of cry

                                                  sister

I couldn't wait the two more weeks
for when we planned to meet
I'm sorry this couldn't be in person
so thank you for taking a moment
from your busy workday
to face time with me
sister you're the youngest
I wish I could hold your hand

> *am I really hearing this now*
> *wait I can't focus*
> *what did she just say*
> *our neighbor across the street!!*
> *the construction worker sand castle weird old guy!?*
> *mom's live-in boyfriend.*
> *MY STEPDAD??*
> *her rancher boss?!*
> *what!! WHAT!!?*

    ohh chris I'm so so sorry please tell me what I can do

I need to ask
did he touch you too
did it happen to you

>   *no*
>
>   no it didn't happen to me

I cry in relief

>   **mom**
>   *maybe my youngest daughter will validate me*
>   *I didn't do anything wrong*

>   **sister**

I've talked to mom
I feel invisible

>   chris I think mom doesn't
>   understand what happened
>   I think she thought he was
>   a nice guy
>   and she was just trying to help
>   someone down
>
>   on his luck

by handing over
her teenage daughter

>   **mom**
>   *but she was*
>   *so DIFFICULT*

                                                                    dad

you left when I was 13 and didn't say goodbye
you don't get to be told by me
not in my voice
that privilege is reserved
for people who were there

                                                            mom
                                            I'm so sorry I failed
                                              I don't know how
                                                I didn't see it

but mom

what about those times
you did see it

the times
when you walked in

and walked away

                              october

                                                                    dad

hey dad
how ya doin'
can you come over
meet me

we'll sit at my picnic table

sure thing chris

there's something you need to know
I've already told the family
I didn't want to tell you
I didn't think
you needed to know
or want to

I've changed my mind
you do

I want you to know
what happened

you're not going to put that on me

THIS ONE I'LL KEEP

it's stuffed down
in the waste paper basket
beside my desk
the only place I could think to put it
to keep it safe
contained
to keep it out of sight
but close
where I could quickly find it
if the missing you hurts too much

when the housekeeper comes
I shove it deep under my desk
file folder box placed in front of it
so clearly it's not trash
they have never touched it

if I touch it too often I'll lose grasp
on the hell-hot days of summers' now
and enter a perpetual winter
but when the missing comes and
I begin to prance and ache
go frantic into flight
for the pains of a phantom limb I lost
the pegasus wing of you
only then do I let myself go

when my fingers forget the feel
the coarse black strands
your mane

I would spend hours untangling
one hair at a time
picking every single twig
every snarl I smoothed
would peel away a layer
off my burden to survive

while you munched your hay
the grinding rhythm of your teeth on time
lulling sound pattern to lean on
the fineness of your coat
a creamy chocolate silk
all in one direction
shining like a candle flame reflection
in an unlit night

I reach into the basket
draw it tenderly out
the ear pockets are torn
it's dirty
caked with hair in the corners
along the noseband
in the creases

we've had dozens of these
fancy ones with ears ordered from catalogs
called state line tack and smart pack and chicks
others plain
picked up from the feed store
where I'd get those crunchy apple treats you liked
the screened mask to keep flies
out of your brown eyes
I close mine

push my face
into the space
where yours had been

inhale you all the way in
this smell of you
like a dog's paw
a spicy underarm
tang of sweetgrass in the wind
with the taste of bone
the breath of home

last november the saturday before thanksgiving
it was damp the gnats were bad
right before I loaded you on the trailer
she'd told me she had one for you
I took it off your face
pulled it gently off your ears
down your long nose
pushing your thick forelock out of your eyes
across your forehead with the fingernail moon star
you placed your muzzle in the cup of my hand
held it there
for the final time
you understand
our silent goodbye
the day I sent you away

the jawbreaking choice only a mother would make
to place you out of harm's reach
to cut the chains from around our feet
to do what needs to be done
I did for you
when it wasn't for me

while I went about the nasty business
of keeping myself alive

WHAT PREVENTED YOU FROM RESCUING ME⁺

she lost hers in a wintertime accident
a snowplow to her driver-side door
freezing out part of her heart
all of her womb

so you were adopted
given away by the smart young nurse
caught in the net
you were told at 7
the age of reason back then
made to promise to keep it secret
until you die

you were 4
when she set you outside
locked out of your house
you remember your fingers reaching
up to the living room window ledge
trying to see inside
wanting to be back in
so bad
what did you do

she beat you with the hairbrush
"just a few times"

you were so fearful
of your younger brother
you would hide
not knowing if the next toaster

or butcher knife would land in you
you were 12 he was 10
where were they I ask
"working I guess" you say

before going out with friends
you had chores
to build a rock garden for the winter's
potatoes and parsnips
dig the pond for your brother's
springtime pet duck
you would take the shovel she held out
cry silently
and dig
sometimes your friends waited
mostly they didn't

brilliant with your interests elsewhere
you were a C student
she fibbed in those college interviews
and said you were an
A
you melted inside your crisp collars
lowered your eyes
your cheeks roasting you alive
like the carrots and beets you chopped
for the family dinners

the time she set you up with the intern
from granddaddy's hospital
at the family table he ate your
meat loaf and potatoes
they all had wine
you sipped your soda pop in silence
and played footsie
with the wolfhounds

how old was he I ask
"29" you say
and how old were you
"16" you say

your dream of joining the red cross died
in the rearview window
as she drove you away to rivier

in college you went the proverbial wild
finally unsupervised and free
without the brother or the chores
you hung the red brassiere
on the blessed mother statue
the flowing stone robe of mary
commanding the quad
it was a dare
and none of the other girls would take it
they laughed at your brazen welcoming you in
with their arms around you
the way hers never did

the backs of her fingers never found
their way to touch your cheeks
her palm never to cup your forehead
or hold your heart tight to hers
never wanting to let you go
you were made to marry dad
being from the right side of the tracks
your equine-loving improper beau
left long behind
forced to be forgotten

five days after your birthday
in september
she turned 50

you'd come home
made a special trip
spending hours in the kitchen
telling her not to come in
baking cupcakes
frosting each one with flair
still warm in your hand
eager to light the candles
and watch the glow
light up her dark-wood eyes
an honor guard of celebration
from a daughter to her mother

her narrowed glare smeared your smile
"how dare you make dumb cupcakes
rather than bake a proper cake!"

you ruined her birthday
drove back with a cold stone
freezing out your heart
and an ocean down your face
so that was why you railed at me
when in perfect naïveté
I baked you cupcakes for your fiftieth
without intending I repeated history
an ingrate is what you called me

our conversation slows
we stroke the dogs under the table
with our bare feet
careful not to touch each other
when did we stop
when were her hands last on my cheeks
I don't remember
exhale low
the reasons why on the table between us
laying messily next

to our coffee cups
cold and going bitter
cream clinging to the rim
congealing

she looks at me
I can barely meet her eyes
my old shame smothering me
slaving ho and heaving hard
to drag me under

so it's this?
this is the why?

I'd told her if I could understand her more
what had got in the way
of her stepping in
between me and them

what had held her back
it would help me
knit myself together again

but now looking at the table
at the list of these whys we've worked so hard
so desperately to retrieve
what she's denied
from the keyhole of her mind
they have no life and lay there limp
no sharpened points that could write me an apology
their flimsy illustration offers no explanation

that can save me

or us

WISH⁺

s elf surrender

u nspeakable

i nvisible

c ollapse

i nstantaneous

d eliverance

e xtinguish

THE YEAR I COLLECTED DOLLS

I am in my bedroom
playing with my dolls
a shadow appears
and it fills the doorway
I stop playing

the memory ends

this young one inside me
the one with the memory
of his shadow

wants to play again

how can I refuse this child

I open my computer
and type etsy in the search bar
hundreds arrive to my
fingertips

which does she want
I let her choose

each month
I let her choose

her delight

that it may return

I can offer dolls
if that is what she wants
and how tender a desire
for a child to want a doll
I can offer dolls

for I cannot offer her
the option to skip that moment
in time's unfolding

it was an enduration
she had to bear
not her choice

I can offer dolls
I will offer dolls
I will let her choose

                                I remember waking from a nap
                              in my nana's house in maine
                       my four-year-old hand holding tight
               to the oak stair rail to toddle my way
                              down the winding case
                                     looking for mom
                          as I round the last curve
                   my eyes begin to bulge and glow
                 and my fist-size heart pounds
                                  and dribbles
                          there at the bottom stair
             sits my mom with smooth cheeks
                                 sparkling eyes
               deep chocolate nut brown hair
           pulled into a lush horse-tail pony
                       and outstretched arms
                             there at her knees
             a miniature scene created from

small books set into table and chair
some stood on end to make a wall
for the dining room
her own girlhood dolls sat having tea
and next to them
their wardrobe closet
with its tiny doors splayed open to
show their change of garments
she'd set this magical scene for
me to find
when I awoke
and she was waiting for me
and we played stories
sprawled side by side on the floor
for two entire days
so inseparable
the love was sealed in

as they arrive
from their earth corners
russia
serbia
america
latvia
england
each month

so does she

the packages held in small hands
the scissors used carefully
to take away the outer
wrappings
brown paper
mailer tape
the label is read many times
then set to the side

a knife once desired
for other purposes
is used to make the vertical slice
down the length of the underbelly
of the box

those small hands fold open
the cardboard
touch the tissue paper blankets
move them to the side
the doll is revealed
her chest swells
this first look fills the
gaping multi-chambered
caverns of her insides
with the blush no less
than a mother's first gaze
the arms extend and reach
for the little one

what courses through the arms
that powers them to lift
the doll
from the past
is not blood but something
older
before the shadow
before the parting seas
before the bloody cross
before the burning bush
before the 40 years of wandering
in the desert
before the dinosaurs
before the big bang
constellated hydrogen atoms

there is something older
that cradles all
carbon
dinosaurs
deserts
those who wander and wonder
bushes on fire
crosses erected
parting seas
shadows that cross bedroom doors

what lifts the arms of all mothers
to hold their children

cradles each of these dolls
handmade
so fresh
full of possibility
of undisturbed play

a rewinding
of the reel

I can offer dolls

at the end of that year
in my forty-ninth
she once again
has an army of dolls
in her arms
her fingertips moving their
small hands to cross their
tiny hearts
twelve miniature shields
set into place

and there will be no more shadows
come to cross her

I invite her back from banishment
to return home to play her cut-short stories
under my own grown power
of protection and peace
the inside child of me

CARDS

when will I know
I've grown
into the woman
I could be

what are the signs
to look for

will they be written
like greeting cards
sent to me
on holidays

will I remember
to send them

MIGRAINE⁺

even the softness of my pillow
enters my skull
like a hammer tip
pushed through
with no mind for the
resistance of bone

I get up
do the regular things

drink down a full glass of water
press the on button to heat the teakettle
I filled last night
open the blinds
pee

I brew tea

a mix of white mui dan
and green kukicha
the sweet grass mixed with dark forest
and cream camellia
lifts me out
for a split second of relief
drops me down roughly
onto my feet
knees buckle slightly
with the hammer pound
the dog doesn't even look up
she knows nothing's out of order

I put my nose into the steeping
hay meadow steam
the hammer comes out my right eye

after the first pour
I lower to the floor
to be more in line
with lali
closer to the ground
is better on these days
cross my legs
put the palm sized cup
to my cheek and temple
the momentary burn
takes all of my attention

after several refills
the pot cools
the burn segments end
and I need to move
the hammer starting through
from the back of my head
headed for my right temporal lobe

once I asked the doctor
if he could see it in my eye
he said no
it's right there I said
pointing to my temple
gesturing to my eyeball

his *no*
but don't worry
they ought to stop
after menopause

made me want
to throw the hammer
at him if I could

I leave the empty cup on the carpet
stand
put my head in the sink
run the tap wide-open cold
inviting double hammer action
but it lasts just a second
then cold-therapy-kindness kicks in
5 - 4 - 3 - 2 - 1

relief is over
with dripping hair
wet pajama top
I open the porch door
and we both go out

I know the drill
exhaust all possible interior
relief hacks
then go outside and look up
scan the sky
come back in
repeat

it's early but past dawn
the sun's still coming up
dabbling adornment through the trees
light pink and gold headdress marbled

I unwrap a light cotton scarf
dyed raspberry pink
from around my head
that I used as compression

it's wet and has a motif
dark brown giraffes running
full tilt free
what are they running from
or to

I lay it out
on a patch of ground
in the shade
the grass needs mowing
I watch a parade of busy ants
march nearby in linear formation
I know they are stronger than humans
maybe they can carry this hammer
out of my head
and bury it deep
wherever ants go
it's wracking the backside
of my eye

I lie down
get pummeled
from the change in plane
I close the curtains of my eyes
press my finger pads
hard in to my brow
force the blood to leave
breathe a while
when I open them
lali is lying only inches away
her presence
a cool hand to my hot cheek
I wouldn't give her the hammer
even if I could
not for anything

I look up

I see the sky is blue
a shade I've never named before
my attention expands
beyond the pain
to identify the blue
of candle flame

I play the cloud game
notice witch-white insides
sting bruise-grey edges
they float and fly by
tumbling from horses into mountains
with anything in between
even hammers of migraines

my outstretched arms shape into a T
bare tricep skin relishing the grass pokies
the hammer commands less of me

I turn my head left
roll to my side
some of me on the scarf
most of me off
I notice those miniature feather ferns
growing between the blades
my right index finger pets one tenderly
it closes daintily
like the ribs of a hand fan
coming up together
the closing of a knife
I shimmer in delight
lali switches to her other side

I keep petting these teeny tiny feathers
until I have caressed them all closed
all the ones I can reach
I roll back onto my scarf

sun's higher and I'm still just barely
under branches canopy

my ears read these words
closed open
clouds clear
sun shade
yin yang
pain ease
joy sorrow
duty desire
hammer feather
dark light
death life

contrasts
opposites

something is coming toward me
barreling down a wormhole
slipped from lips high above
knowledge gnosis
slams its whisper into me
dust rises in a cloud puff
a compete set of encyclopedia
would be too small to contain
the simplicity of it ridiculous
the complexity of it explodes
supernovas my brain
purnamadayah
catalyzing my understanding
into words held in my hand
I can read like braille

I couldn't be more awe struck
if the sky began to snow

in one long run-on
sentence supra stuffed
a bulging bubble
entered me

the gift of life is duality
balancing bevel the scales of justice
level contrast's illusion origin
for dark and light combine
as equal thread
knit the eros night and hadic white
connective tissues of rotations
our body galactic
fascia rise and fall
push and pull the tidal wall
even though wave illusory
out of oceans' all
the gift of life
is duality

it ricocheted inside me
sculpting river's thunder
naming unnamed oceans
fresh trawled blood lanes
brand my skin
replace the hammer
cast it down
sizzle away the last shreds
of my sense consensus
and rose me upright sitting

lali too
she thinks we are going in
and it's time to eat
the sun is beaming out
up past the old oak high tops

fern fans have reopened
the ants gone on about
their daily business
my hair is dry
the shade has disappeared
rising we take to the stairs
for her breakfast
for my journal
for the pen I need

to write
this
down

but my eyes track movement
my feet stalling in mid step
across the yard
a rabbit
goes hopping by
stops a second
to nibble on a clover
under a solitary single
flake of snow

HERD MEDICINE

Dear Wren,

You were an emaciated, long two-year-old bay Thoroughbred, already seventeen hands high. That's sixty-eight inches tall at the withers, the arch where the neck joins the back. I took one look at your bony body with your head hung low and said yes. It was high time to get another horse. I was a newlywed bride living in a rented farmhouse and lonely with my husband traveling out of town almost weekly for work. I spent all of my time with you, Wren, and you thrived under my care and attention. The house sat on one hundred acres of fallow farmland and woods. We roamed and rode all over the landscape. We swam the ponds together. While you grazed, I spent hours studying the property we inhabited. We took walks in the evenings, sometimes single file, sometimes side by side. I began listening again. I changed from using steel-bitted bridles to bridles with no bit. Alongside you, my body began to fall into a rhythm it seemed to be remembering as if from another life.

One late morning in autumn, we found ourselves in a yet undiscovered meadow, and even you were surprised. An entire sea of monarch butterflies covered the land like a shimmery sheet of orange-and-black iridescence fluttering through the air. As we rode slowly through the field, the butterfly wings touched my face, landed on my arms and on your ears. I was kissed all over by the flickering air. The memory engraved itself into my heart and infused my blood.

Wren, you and I were nearly inseparable. Anytime I left on a trip, you would get yourself into some kind of puzzle. You'd get a leg caught in the fence; get yourself trapped lying down, too tight against your stall; get caught under a tree limb hanging too low for your height; or have a stomachache. You would never fight or get into a panic. You'd patiently wait to be untangled, freed, or soothed from your predicament. I would invariably get the call, and I'd let you know with a letter on the ethers that I was coming home and you'd right yourself straightaway without a hitch or fuss.

Ideas and visions for helping others learn to listen to themselves by being listened to and heard by horses emerged out of me, but always through you. I designed and launched workshops and residential retreats highlighting horse listening and the healing that comes from companioning a horse. During this time, you began to coax me out from the underground, where I'd long taken refuge.

Inexplicably, you became ill with a bilateral lung disease. You were in and out of hospitals for over a year. I would record messages that your vets would play for you when I couldn't be there. When you were finally able to come home, I moved you to my mom's because I knew I would need her help with the grueling hospice-like schedule your care now required. I quit my work. My life was you. In Chinese medicine, lung ailments represent sadness. Wren, were you embodying what I still refused to acknowledge in myself? You stayed alive for another twelve months.

When it was finally your time, and the will of my dedication and the force of my love for you could no longer keep you here, you lay down to die. The example of your fearless grace facing death riddled my bones with a loss that to this day I cannot describe. My dad gave me a long nail spike he spray-painted gold, and I hammered it high into a tree near your grave to mark where you lie. It is still there. I wore a red string around my wrist for an entire year.

Thank you, Wren, my big boy, beloved one. I feel you near with your great Pegasus-angel wings; you are not forgotten.

Love,

Christin

SOUTH TEXAS LAZARUS[+]

shoot straight down 35

crack your windows and inhale

acres in the hundreds are swathed

in fresh cut carpet green

pallets stacked hat high

with grass san augustine

strong cocoa arms of suntanned workers

mismatched to their wet denim blue

sweat stained backs

the air is mossy sweet

mingling with the new mown

coastal bermuda next farm over

take a left on highway 60

to fly by fields

some with ancient windmills

some boasting upgrades

sporting the slow sweep and whoosh

of turbine blades as the wind farms encroach

if you keep going and don't brake

the sand dunes will soon stop you

and you can stroll directly

into the gulf of mexico

where the iced tea colored waters

beachcomb the shore

and ruffle your bare feet in foam

flooded rice fields

open temporary lagoons

a breakfast oasis to saber beaked

blue feathered hunters

making silver filleted quick tapas

of short lived minnows

you drive by snowy summer fields

millions of two inch tiny

ice white bolls

individually wrapped

in their foliage packages

beckon you to stop

half your tires overlap the edge

of the sloped shoulder

the car almost still rolling

you throw the door open

and dash to the field

to pick one then another and another

staring at these mini marvels

and how these fuzzy puffs

in your palm

transform into your tee shirt

humidity blots

your underarms rorschach

on down the road

a john deere green combine

takes up backcountry lanes

in both directions

flashing lights caution

a slowdown

his wide berth lumbers over

and you can just scoot by

to answer his waving hand

yours goes up too

speaks the same silent word

in the rearview

the gesture brings a smile

we're a momentary team

and doing things together

like sharing the road

is how we live out here

barbed fencing unwinds fast

at seventy miles an hour

painterly shapes in blacks browns greys creams and reds

dab and dash the landscape

heads curled down to graze

or grouped in the corners

where chinaberry junk trees often root

to rest and soak in mid-noon shade

the cows' knees buckle together

bending low to the ground

as if at first to bow

before lying down to pray

they chew their cuds

while the horses stand

their tails circling slow

to keep biting insects

off their bellies

white cattle egrets linger near

to chop stix the flies

beaks faster than wings

field by field

the miles slip past

the ground territory

changing slow constellations

lulling your shoulder muscles supple

tension drifts away on the wind

with the windows rolled down

the southern heat billows the interior

with steamy fingers

your cola can in the console

beads up as its cold disappears

along with the moisture in your skin

being drawn up by the same sun

that touches the canopy fringe

of hip width wide sycamores

with the bronze and silver leaves

boosting them higher each season

circling high all afternoon

mississippi kites lace a beeline for locusts

their stringing wing sound violining

when the buzzing stops you know

they've become early suppers

an inland sea of botany

in a yellow brick road profusion

of black top-hatted shoulder-padded gold

a flower hour to outline

the highway home

a cloud maze of round baled hay

dot and star

the upside down sky as I go by

texas pink evening primrose

furry with pollen

alive in a hive of drunk busy bees imbibing

after daytime retires for the night

you might look up and spot the big dipper

or a fingernail moon

feel your presence begin to shrink

and a certain kind of homelessness moves in

light pricked darkness both edgeless and ageless

outfits you in transient loneliness

fitting like a set of clothes not bought for you

but if you listen for the remaining

locust song and exhale long

that'll set you right again

everyone around here knows

the witching hour isn't midnight

it begins one hour earlier

when all the town stoplights

start to blink yellow and continue their winking

all night long

exactly when us kids would appear

to cruise up and down

the one main drag

we'd laugh and point at each other

eat tacos and never suspect

the march of adulthood approaching

but the best transformations

are the splotchy brown resurrection ferns

that cover the arms of the pin and live oaks

their parched and curly frills

appear mostly dead and crunchy

when one day we'll have a quenching rain

and on the morning after

you'll view a magic show

the stoic oaks tricked out

draped in such shiny velvet finery

that all you want to do is

dress your fingers down

the now dewy

lazarus lichen

is no longer siphoned near death dry

or prematurely taken

it's temporarily been given back

a gift unto itself

a promise restored

a life returned

I AM NOT

your toy
your doll
your pen pal
your thing
your bitch
your victim
your fantasy
your slave
your little friend
your call girl
your dirty secret
your fuck doll
your late night ride
your reject
your last resort
your little experiment
your project
your backup

keeping your secrets

yours

IT WAS PREARRANGED[+]

you drove the hour and a half south and east / toward the gulf / where I grew up / climbing those old oaks with so many highway boughs to choose from / body surfing shrimp boat and oil rig churned up waves / collecting stringy spanish moss to build spidery tumbleweeds / riding ponies / half horses then tall horses and fences / reaching into my limbs / as they are today / but this day I stayed in the city / those legs pacing me through our spare span of rooms / lali following me like we're hosting a tiny parade / the banners waving "this day is a first" / and the floats swathed in black crepe / instead of blowing party foam / they'd spew cremation dust / the candy tossed would rot your teeth in days / it's too early to expect your call / I carry the phone anyway / ringer on high / I eye the edradour / scotch in the hutch / it's 9:42 on Sunday morning / it was after church / that schedule stayed the same / you'd tell me later / you didn't even rehearse what you'd say / didn't need to / the words / they'd been etched inside you / the first time I told you / 9 years after we married / your mouth had hung open / as I rattled on like I was telling you about who I saw / at the grocery store yesterday / my tone and words not matching the story stuck in my body / the same one that climbed / surfed / and rode / that body but not this body / couldn't be / they met you at the back door holding coffee / an extra cup poured ready for you / a powwow / a quick review in between gulps / no time for cream / no sugar / you were going to get his attention / praying he'd be outside / tending his flowers / the zinnias so pretty / from across the street / blueberry blue / cloak purple / kitchen yellow / teenage-girl pink / they lingered / trailing behind as planned / my mother and my brother / but would stay behind you / stand at the end of the driveway / make a row across the gate / giving you space / but close enough to serve as the body of proof / he was outside / touching those innocent petals / he must've looked up / with that wide open face / teeth bumping mustached lips / to shape a neighborly smile and friendly hello / you were going to say / I need to talk to you / a minute / come into the street / waving him over to where clipped grass meets asphalt / and the toes of your power-stanced feet / I wonder once he saw you / did it begin to creep in / my family's faces / a solid line of conviction / it wasn't discussed / but my oldest brother / began filming / iphone steadied lengthwise on the top edge of the gate / to catch every single second / of this about to go down / when I watched this video / late that night / that edradour trembling / in my hand / what struck me most / was the height of him / standing in front of you / on even ground / you are the same size / he did not tower stories over you / the way my memory swore it / during all the replays all these decades / even only last year / when he crossed the street / to *say hello* when I was getting from her box / my mother's mail / I *know* I looked up / my head tilting back / so far back onto my neck / the only way I could meet his face with mine / I swear he'd been sky high / your shoulders are solid / turned squarely at him / I can imagine I hear / *if you ever* / you can see the exact moment it strikes him / the blank horror of truth / coming to bathe him / in accountabilities boiling oil / the way he's mopping his brow / he's dying alive in it now / I know this is when you are saying / the part about / *we all know what you did to christin for all of those years / and those sick fuck letters you wrote / she found them / we have them /* the video is mostly silent / it being recorded 15 feet away / but it screams inside my head / every single word / no water / no ice / I sip more than a sip / and ask out of character / for a second two fingers / as I swallow / the grateful burn chokes on how no one has / ever / ever / ever / ever / stood for me / in front of me / up for me / until now / and as I look into your eyes / the video ended / I can't speak the three words / that race with the bile / coming up from my gut / all those years / that I've misplaced / my hate of him / of all of them / *onto you dear husband* / and you have carried it so stoically / your compassion and your wisdom / eclipsed the cannon fire I launched at you / because you were the first safe man in my life / and a place where I could put it / but now I curl close to you / bring my lips to your ear / one hand to your heart / and with all of mine /

I whisper / *I'm so sorry*

APPLE

standing there holding the knife
hips holding up the counter
the sliced-apple smell
its fresh-parted flesh white
with reddish burnt-pink rim
a solitary stem
plucked clean out

transports me years
behind me
reminds me of my own too-soon-ness
being caught between his hands
pared into pieces for his eating pleasure
crispy and ripe
seeds still tight
stolen out from the garden
walked out through the unlocked gate
in the palm of his hand

tossed up and down
high in the air
each time the catching
a loud slap against the shiny skin
snatching of a good girl

bought with a sleazy smile
a bottle of wine
and a handful of wilted red carnations
the green tissue wet
from his sweaty fingers

concealing the way he'd use them
later like weapons
cleaving me open
alone
behind a locked door
his free hand covering my no

back in the kitchen
the softening glow
of low west light
shines in my eye
I see the red smear growing
across the cutting board
from my unfelt finger
covering the apple I was about to eat
it looks ready and good
except for the stain I'm giving it

was it that easy slicing me open

the apple lies in my hand
still bleeding

FIREFLIES FLASHLIGHTS AND HORNED TOADS

1.

they have disappeared
nearly
I didn't notice their leaving
the when
there's no map point to pin to
the moment
no story to describe the how
I just noticed one night
their absence

I began to tremble
how you start to know something
a small feeling
in a single cell
vibrates the walls of it
until cells surrounding
start to tremble too
transfer electrical physical
sensation though the maze
of your body
to the surface of your skin
that tiny tremble
a soft cymbal
a clang in your heart
that click in your head
shaking now
in the shape of your shoulders
your jaw clamped closed

like a fist
or howled open palmed wide
in a suspended hung silence
so painful
no sob can leave

the minute I realized they were gone
flashed for what seemed like always
and my autonomic missing
of them for decades
the never having named their loss
reduced me
to the denominator uncommon
the horrible sum
of their goneness

2.

I used to play with them
didn't you
those little bulbs of pulsing light
darting through backyards
after supper
little-people-sized butterfly nets
and the empty jars
would come out of closets
wait on the ground
nestled just right
to stay upright between the grass tufts
lids nearby close to hand
those little lanterns
a soliloquy to dark time dances
performed with charms
I longed to decipher
giggling delight peppered imaginary parchment
with the disappearing ink
of my childhood

we released them
but sometimes not soon enough

in daytime I'd mount up
his saddle no higher than your waist
buckle on my brother's toy gun and holster
and in a tumbleweed of little girl and pony
we'd ride off hell-bent ready to explore
and play stories
I'd get in trouble with mom
for losing that holster
making my brother cry
I went back for days after
looking but it was lost
we called them the hills
really grown-up dump truck
loads of foundation dirt and sand

                                              exactly like the one
                                            that one day he and I
                                      would be parked behind
                                      in his wife's red truck
                                  me horizontal in his lap
the console radio the lonely only
                                                  peacock blue
                                   neon candle of the night

waiting for the neighborhood
to expand
with houses just like mine

I was intent to round up
all the imaginary bad guys
never guessing that not long later
they would emerge for real

at the hills I found
miniature dinosaurs
toads with horns
armor decorating their necks and bodies
tiny collars and corsets of pokey bones
made great little handles
for picking them up
my thumb and forefinger held their skeletons
that seemed to be on the outside
where they didn't belong
their soft little bellies hanging down
I gathered and collected them
into makeshift chutes and holding pens
I built from twigs and rocks
I'd read them their rights
you have the right to remain silent

teddy grazing nearby
his teeth shearing off clover cluster tops
paying no attention to me and my imagination
I never kept the little dinos
corralled for long
they looked so miserable huddled together
my game would abruptly end
I'd carefully place them
where I'd found them
retracing my steps
so they could each find their way
back home
I would watch
as they all popped
safely inside their burrows

a tickle would start in my heart
pumping its legs low and slow
like it was enjoying the longest arc
you can make in a swing

it painted a rainbow the color of rapture
the pot of gold my ticker
gilding my bones in grace gratitudinal
for their little bony
bodies
what mysteries
the joy that these little bony bodies
amen existed at all

then it would be time to eat supper
could just hear mom's calling coming
through the telephone lines of oak limbs
I'd mount up quickly ignoring the stirrups
my little hand ahold of the horn
I'd fly myself up through the air
land lightly in the saddle
hightail it home across the circle
wending through empty lots
waiting for their houses
families and fences

3.

standing here now
looking out
my mother's kitchen window
sea glass shells and feathers
pieces of soap leftover dog biscuit
the tiny orchid pink and chartreuse
I gave her
growing with glee despite her self-described unwieldy thumb
compete for space on the altar of her sill

I've come to visit
we make a plan for pancakes
tomorrow morning once she gets home
from church

she sets the table pats her folded napkins
counts out loud the tablespoons to brew our coffee
I brown the bacon in the oven
listen for the sizzle
cakes on the griddle
wait for the bubbles
I look around the kitchen
everything the same
without the register of my brain
nothing has changed
from those days to these
I fiddle with the dial to turn down the heat
except everything

my pilot light blew out
thirty years before
that I'd felt
but it was their goneness
my daytime friends the tiny dinosaurs
the every evening flicker chorus
that I could not bear to see
not there
even though I've looked a thousand times
and was still looking

star-cut shapes prick the velvet cape of night
some skeletons still do dangle
on the outside of closed doors
and tied to my thoughts they clink
and tinkle softly

the harsh light flashed
from the metal can he palmed
spotlighting across the street each night
this was not the glow-dust pulse
of my faerie flies I loved so well
instead his ogre-gazing flashlight

                          was winking out his spell
                     letting me know he was watching
                                 looking for me
                            eyeing me with that laser
                            his letter code spelling me
                              each one telling me
                    I'm spotted even when I'd skirt behind
                 trees on the way from the barn to the house
                                he watched me
                                 keeping track
                      later in letters he'd write what I'd worn
                  the zigged rainbow of my pink floyd tee shirt
                            hiding behind the moon
                           I didn't want to take them
                          he pushed them into my hand
                         closing his fist around my fingers
                               to curl them closed

                                   don't tell

                            their origami branding me

4.

my hands automatically
soap themselves
ablutional instinct
bubbles sud into the sink
to purify my fingerprints
wash my skeletons' secrets
tinkling bones
down the drain

in the split spark of a second
a low groan inside my mouth
blooms across my chest
a lit match

sounding like the color ocher
hard-slap purple
the red of bricklayers' hands

beloved horned toads
I read how the fire ants
stole your lives
every one eaten alive
your tiny armor no defense

the fireflies
lost themselves to the sky
crop dusting behind our house
blew their breath away
I cry for the loss I could not see

they death marched
the grief of my childhood
into markerless graves
the wasteland
where all innocence goes

PANCAKES+

the batter was loose
the color of ripe lemons
until he added the vanilla
it alone would have you
running down the stairs
or in from the yard
to find a place at the table
you couldn't buy it in the store
back then it came straight from mexico
in a glass liter bottle
with a red rooster on the neck
seemed like he'd crack a hundred eggs
and whir them silly
until the batter turned gold
he'd hold the side of the silver bowl
his thumb just touching the batter
high over the frying pan
crackling hot with oil
pour enough in to cover the whole bottom
once the top began to mutter and bubble
he'd take his favorite
palm-sized slatted spatula
shaped like a fan
to create that restaurant secret
and circle round and under
the entire pancake rim and make
the perfect grill cake ring
one after the other
manna cakes the color
of mixed warm honey and butter

grew fairytale high
stacked like dinner plates
steam rising through the flour sack cloth
a white banner to hungry bellies
at the table we'd be seated
and before our hands shot out for the platter
he'd say "let's sing like the devil for the lord!"
and we'd chorus back "amen!"
like flying saucers we'd whirl them
through the air across the table
aiming for the open doors
of our toothy smiles
slather cheap butter like frosting
over the golden cake tops
caramel sugar syrup the final heavy grace
watch it decorate the sides in frothy loops
we'd fork and knife them into shapes
kaleidoscope tiles on our plates
spear four or five pieces all dripped in sweet
disappear them behind mmm-ing mouths
pancakes for supper on Sundays
still try to make home feel safe

CITIZEN

I have created my new self
my language
my country
cities farms and towns
traditions and parliamentary procedures
I contain the citizens of myself

my own mother nature
the blood of my constitution
tornados hurricanes monsoons
trade winds
rippling grasses
herds of wild horses
buffalo

brazen new territory of me
newly discovered property
I have purchased
with my own ripped insides
hanging them out
from veins
pins on a clothesline
spelling out
I
love
you

my lonely old highways
ancient with crimson cobwebs
newly driven

by the wheels of my own
turning body
I wield fresh life
of me
out from the old
wreckage
broken angled limbs
torn hair
mangled heart
queen of me recovered
my jewels remembered
memory gems
I am my own
my mother and my father

I am god
I am the father
I am goddess
I am the mother
nature born of myself
out of the womb of I

I am the covenant of the rainbow

never understood before
unsettled body and unsung tears
that morphed into loneliness and loss of
direction come dawn
I understood they did not come from me
but only through me
a world apart in difference
a relief
origin and expression
an explosion
chasing my long lost first birth
elusive goblet of effervescence
bubbles frothy with the lift of ideas

like millions of tiny little eggs
all pink and cream

this grail I chased
highly guarded secret this
my new me
a rough cut of dirt diamond and pearly tourmaline
I am birthed
again and again each day
by my own permission

I dress her up
wrap strands of small oysters
about her willowy neck
to tally the pearls of her laughter
and let her run
naked on tiptoes
through the dappled shadows of her
body's countryside
glowing under
cover of clouds
playing hide and seek with the moon

I cloak her in crimson azure
river and night
I send her into battle
armed with warrior weapons
razor tongue and wit and woman stem
warring with the others of her
reigning for this day
revel in the aftermath smoky with casualty

or I can choose to sit beside her
skin the color of bitten peach
tattooing my shoulder and
absorb the talent
of her life

my breath
like bread sponging her up

I have realized I am more
than first believed
the container of myself does not fit
into the shape of a wheel and go only
in one direction

it's a non containment
I am world with no end
of my own choice
making and design
self-appointed queen maker
I am my own brazen tender love child

my sky is not only blue but robin's-egg-ocean-midnight
breath is not just breath but cloud cream
a simple step is the very leap of hanuman
to run is to be like golden eagle flight
with powerful horse-wild limbs
I realize now
with outstretched arms
woven with life lines
glimmering gold like bracelets
the sacrificial girl

strapped to the gear of a life
survived alive with new meaning
self unshackled now
laid aside in pink pillow shroud
with a wrenching grace
a small wave and one backwards glance

I am the unnamed planet
discover me

THE FIFTH⁺

to you unnamed

and unknown number five

fleshed out during trance and song

unconscious knowing

held checkrein tight too long

be damned

I'm onto you

I know you're out there

and you know who you are

my memory will haunt your quick

slowly saw it open

peck it to the bone

for your mortal marrow

and will feed it

to las cucarachas

HERD MEDICINE

Dear Mission,

It had been over a year and I was still saying I wasn't ready for another horse even as we pulled up to the corral and parked. A tall chocolate-brown off-the-track Thoroughbred with a black mane lifted his head. The crescent moon on your forehead flashed when your forelock shifted from the movement. I saw you looking at me with curious eyes. Though they were rich brown, they were peculiar. I could see the sclera. The whites of horses' eyes usually only show when spooked or hyperalert, and though your body appeared calm, you looked haunted. I didn't understand it at the time, but I recognized that look.

I never carry treats or carrots around horses. That way, when a horse comes to share personal space with me, I always know it's because of me and not the carrot. And here you came. Your current owners were saying you were dangerous. You walked directly to me and sniffed my hand over the fence, whiffling your nostrils to say hello. Staring open-mouthed at us, your owners said, "He's not a safe horse, but if you want him, you can have him."

I retrieved the bit-less bridle I had with me in the truck, for "just in case." I entered the pasture; you came over and lowered your head. I slipped the bridle gently over your soft chocolate ears. Throwing caution to the wind, I climbed onto you bareback and asked for the gate to be opened. We headed down the driveway easy as pie. We took a few trots up and down the country road. I asked you for a halt. You stopped. As we rode back toward the people and their house, every cell in your body seemed to vibrate loud enough for me to hear "My name is Mission, and you need to take me home." My body tingled back to answer you: *Yes*.

I got you home, and as the settling-in weeks passed, the dreamlike reverie we had shared began to break apart. I started to understand what the people had been saying. Your movements became explosive and unpredictable. At any moment, you could go from walking quietly on the lead line, standing peacefully being groomed, or even resting or grazing out in the pasture to twisting yourself into a shattering tornado. The heaving violence of your body shredded the oxygen from the air and soaked me in adrenaline.

These spells seemed to come out of nowhere. You were terrifying. Once my forearm was struck by your flailing hind hoof. The smacking sound was so loud it stunned me completely, and for many moments I did not feel the pain. In an instant, my arm tripled in size. I cradled it with my other hand and I fled to the house for ice. As I ran, my thoughts came in slow motion: *This horse is showing me my own terror and rage, when will I finally listen?*

Unbelievably, you didn't break my arm. But you had literally forced my hand and demanded my reckoning. In that moment our true love affair began. I knew it was time to find my way back to myself, the one I had been denying all these decades. We made an agreement that if I finally took responsibility for myself and my feelings, you would never hurt me. You never exploded again. We went on to delight in many years of performing together at liberty, in the privacy and comfort of the back pasture.

Even though you are gone now, I still feel you out there. From the star-spangled freedom of your angelic realm, I am aware of you circling me, encasing me in an arc of protection.

Thank you.

Love,

Christin

WHAT IF I'D BECOME A CHERRY CLERK[+]

honey washing coffee beans
for my art and dime
would I have loved these horses
like I do

or how rolling in clover
wild strawberry and winter hay
feels to my skin and bones
its prickly softness
tickling my heart

I might not have had chickens
I named margaret jinks and raisinette
carrying them under my arms
to go check the mail
into the house
put the mail on the counter
grab an apple
from the dog-gnawed basket
in the kitchen

never would have known
chickens take their baths in dirt
would have missed the delight
of their necks writhing underneath them
to ruffle the softest soil into places
they can't reach with their beaks
their eyes half closed
wings stretched out to sun
I might have lived at the end of a road

where people missing the highway exit
would turn around

not on a circle with one way in and one way out

I'd have missed braiding manes
late at night
standing on a stool
while the horses slept
gently swishing their tails
lips lipping grain bits missed
using cobwebs to twist tie
the plaited ends together

their muffled nickers
and yawns
translate ease and safety

I might have missed the morse code
of fireflies in the night fields
sending dictation to the sky

I can follow my nose blind
to either sycamore or ponderosa pine
the manure pile
into the tack room to put my hand
on leather

rather than post-roast
aroma and taste
of chocolate nutmeg
rubber white flower maple sugar

sausage raisin or sour lime
coffee couture sublime

if I'd become a cherry clerk

or anything else but me

STAY

two obituary versions float
orbit my mind in alternating rings

while I'm having morning tea
with my dog and journal meditation

when I'm walking on the beach
pause to inspect a shell
a bit of sea smooth glass

with my wrists soapy and warm
washing dishes to pristine

after chopping vegetables into rounds
moons small dice or cube
for salad or stir fry or soup

on the yoga mat to remain limber
ebbing firm
strengthen muscles
elongate my spine

driving the highway midline
dash dash dash

after a belly laugh with a neighbor
in the street her mail in her hand

the two versions seesaw and merry-go-round
fall off the monkey bars

get back up
they tap me on the shoulder
I wonder which one

Version 1
―――――

Christin Marie Staszesky
departed and took to the sky
the same day she entered it
fifty years before

it was an accident

she was alone
having left her lali
behind at home that day
her note said she was ready
for this solo hike
she'd been planning
for fifteen years
her body was fit and fine
her books and journals
her nature love letters
dusted and rearranged
dog food bought
supper preps left with post-it
notes for what to do

Drain the miracle noodles
Warm the pecorino mushroom sauce
Combine gently
Add chopped chicken
Salt to taste

Enjoy
I love you

she'd been looking forward
talked about it
she loved nature
the beach
the forest
the sky
the stars

loved to walk dirt roads with her dog
pick up acorns
seed pods
feathers

her first passion was horses
they beat her heart
their hooves rippled
the ocean of her blood
in their company
she was happy

for a while

her purpose was service
authenticity her number one value
the compass she lived by
helping others rise from their knees
to bushwhack and seed their own path
to healing repair and recovery
she synergized her chosen fires
horses and healing
together
to create another choice for people
to explore
a lens to see through

a new way to feel liberty
inside their soma body

these braided pathways
restored world meaning
having vanished 30 years before
after the crossing of
her bodylines

she had few friends
the ones she had
claimed her loyalty
and a fierce dedication
to maintain closeness and care
she loved to give gifts
and her chosen sangha
often found
sweetly wrapped tiny
packages on their porches
people mattered

grief shaded in shallows
darkened the skin below
her eyes
turned it purple
the bruise of depression
we saw but chose not to
assigned it instead to the weariness
of migraine ownership

never dreaming . . .

her loss surprises us
how could we not have seen
through the wide smile
we came to lean on for light
at times when light was low

destroys those of us
who find empty now
the shape that was hers
alone

we will from now on miss
her familiar silhouette
inner strong contour
we hope she has found
the peace that eluded
her here

Version 2

we celebrate the long
thrill of life
this intriguing
woman of style service
and gladness
Christin Marie Staszesky

though there are few of us here
she lived so long
those of us who are
relish and delight
this beauty lived until threadbare

what a shine she threw
from her eye
the corner of her mouth
she could lift a thousand pounds
with the force of her kindness
dedication to service to people
was the torch that lit the halo

of hearts in people who found
their way home by the outstretched
palm she offered without reserve
a hole through the middle of it

her niece turned 13 and was safe
from unbidden eyes hands mouths
and worse

in her early years she overcame
an adversity many face and fail
to return from
a coal of grit remained lit
to inspire and kindle
the bonfire of will
to recover her body
from the premature grave
she might have dug
as many do
and have done

her niece turned 14 and was safe
from unbidden eyes hands mouths
and worse

she loved people
especially strangers
who often would not remain so
she loved to laugh
and did so more and more
in her later years
there was a freedom in her gait
we swore she was a dancer
she always swore back
that no
it was something else

a lifetime yogini?

still something else she'd say

riding horses your whole life?

still something else she'd say

it was the decision to stay

her niece turned 15 and was safe
from unbidden eyes hands mouths
and worse

we read in a book she wrote
that capped her fiftieth year
to save her own life
and in the hope of others too
even one

she built this life
around the one she did
not think she'd have
until after the decision

she chose roses
only varieties that you could smell
the kind that would invite
your steps to slow
to pause
lean over
lift their heads to your nose
inhale
deeply and again

planted herbs
parsley

thyme
oregano
culantro
aztec herb sweeter than sugar

she chose herbs to lift life into
the waters she drank
the pestos of ireland green

she chose vegetables in midlife
instead of . . .

turned the earth by hand
dug each individual little burrow
by the same hand she held out
to those who had nowhere else
to turn with their own
heaving hollowed out hearts
and sucked dry bones

those tender edibles grew
along the driveway
and grew
and she celebrated
life by harvesting her miniature crop
ate salad

her niece turned 16 and was safe
from unbidden eyes hands mouths
and worse

what was this life in the city
country girl found herself in
arrived there on the magic carpet
of both love and wreckage
the struggle of her own history
crushing her against the ropes

in the corners
face down on the mat
the countdown begun
bleeding from everywhere
the grief of crossed body borders
the past still haunting
the present
she chose compromise
instead of . . .

she chose to accept reality
instead of . . .
she chose to prevail
instead of lose

her niece turned 17 and was safe
from unbidden eyes hands mouths
and unspeakably worse

her journals cradled her observations
her nieces' nubile bodies
burgeoning
blooming
bursting forth from childhood
studded with tight smooth skin
curves coming out of baby pudge
flowers unfolding their petals
in no rush
bathe in their fresh glory
from girls
into young women
who think they know
the pearl in the oyster is theirs

her niece turned 18 and was safe

from unbidden eyes hands mouths
and unspeakably worse

they each had been her

HER!
HER!
HER!
HER!
HER!
HER!
HER!
HER!

each eight one at a time

innocent and unsuspecting
young beautiful does trotting
in slow motion
through fields
both tart spring and high wintered grass
because they can and for the joy
of the feel of willowy stems tickling
underbellies
what could they know of the horrors
that might lurk
and leer their way

it will not happen to them
what is not widely known
is the other half of
the world is your oyster
shakespeare also wrote
it must be opened
by sword

and Christin
she has
opened it by sword
as she was opened

her basket of childhood
pearls were spilled
she spent the rest of her life
gathering them all back

she understood suffering
was sacred
she came to respect it
honor it
and yes
to love it

her nieces turned all the ages she
had been
and were safe
because she chose
to speak

to stay

SOBER

with arteries drenched
in alcohol not blood
I could have been a drunk
shot up with one-way tracks
locked in a hospital
lost under a bridge
stoned out of my mind
with no address

at least it wouldn't feel
like this

but no
I chose another path
and have been the shell
shocked somber witness

the only chalice to touch my lips
ran with grief and the raw gnashing
of my teeth
the only needle I ached for finding
to sew and seam myself
to knit my ripped
through fencing
ravaged rented bodyline
lay unfindable in the hay

I chose instead to suffer
sober with my suffering
long until the night

I was rendered unfrozen
re membered home together
by my holy honey
and re minded my soul's
sacrosanct sobriety

and in the day
I found that needle in the hay
and struck one prick
through its eye
my new storyline
a girl of glimmering gold

A COLLECTION OF LOVE LETTERS

my bones lengthen and shorten
when I watch my altar
from the tip of a long tooth
that long downhill nasal slope
painted white thunderbolt
covering one nostril
how it ends in a muzzle
so articulate and fine
it can choose between
single blades of grass

my arm bones leg bones tiniest finger bones
extend from the longing of my heart bones
remembering those muzzle lips nibble

pluck the pinecone from the soles
of my feet
I bring it to my eye
to see what's in there
all the letters hung on tiny shingles
when I twirl it
the alphabet shakes out
into my hands
I can read the lines of my story

the bulbul waves his red flag
jay and wren stop to listen
nod yes to my altar tending

where my palms scribe
hallowed screen play
I do enact
out loud and boldly
with no rehearsal

then they fly away
dropping one large raptor feather
in applause

I pull it from my hair
place it on the puja where it gets to know
angel-shaped prayers of others
each object a miniature ceremony
of my nature in the mirror
directed with both wand and clapboard

intact bleached-white lizard skeleton
preserved a year under the front door mat
vertebrae bones of cow deer elk
some I spray paint gold

tiny chili peppers were left
that time I asked a question
to go forward or stop
those spicy runes spelled the sign to continue
chiles dried up from my joy squeezing out

swallowtail wing to meet pinyon pine sap ball
they waltz around
two possum jaws tied fast together with care
using leftover girl-pink
present ribbon
butterfly wing and waxy liquor dancers
collapse in a love heap
near the quartz crystal moon and the paper wasp hive
each catacomb a perfect circle

of sacred geometry
a gasp of light escapes me
my lips transform into
upward facing fingernail moon

in the backyard
I stack mortars as tall as my waist
centuries etched to their bowls
each the size of my belly
underneath the camphor canopy
they advertise as high rise housing
solitary cinnamon brown rabbit
claims the bottom floor
her tiny "this is home" sign
tickles my rib case
I unroll my company of spine bones
onto weed-dotted lawn
henbit and dandelion my cushions
clover pillows my head crowned
with sky kissing the ground
I gaze up through closed curtains
my eyelids taking a nap
the daytime stars peep through

ether silk spiral giggles next to my ear
tap out code to my heartbeat
and hearing the next steps
will pencil the directions
to the inside of my mouth
where my tongue will write them
longhand down my horse's neck

I will read them strand by strand
and never be lost again

BREATHWORK

when breath comes
to offer its gusto cape
to the intimate insides of you

it's one size fits all
and somehow
is the exact dimension
no matter your person

on your back
made friendly with pillows
a blanket at your feet
sitter stationed nearby
for any coming need
a drink, a tissue
escort to the bathroom

you raise the mask
silk cotton or bamboo
to cover your eyes
and signal the inception

you enter
the canoe alone
push off from the bank
of this topside land
and soon surrender the paddles
back to the dock
for they will no longer

afford aid or help pilot
where you are going

boundary-less landscape
where the borders
don't encircle underneath
their continuance

but drop off into
empty space pits
pointing you
toward a mapless expanse
where no footprint
can be found

it does not negotiate
the timing of its arrival
or the volume of its wind

the breath spirals through
your interior heartland
stoking its bellows
your chest and belly
puff and blow

from your memories
reveries and destinies
it picks up what it wants
to show you backstage
behind your closed eyes

it will play with
your limbs
and bid directions
projected from the inside
enacted into tangled visions
crystal refractions

a pantomime display
choreographed
of past or future
a present course explained
in an unknowable language
yet understood
by your heart and you
its actor and actress

you can be tempted
to stop the procession
its presence
can become too much

you could
simply stop breathing
but if you do
you know you will
destroy
this one-time momentary
viewing of yourself
the arms of animation
will never hold you again
quite this way

this kaleidoscope proof
will shatter itself
if the portal closes
to bar its marching call

you keep the door open
and whistle the signal
whisper again to your breath
flay yourself open
to it
keep going in
and in

and in
in

until you are no longer doing it
the breathing
but being it
and it becomes
your doer

its hand over yours
the reins slacken
and it carries you forward
where you cannot go
where you long to go
you sail
the swells
of it

the breath knell peals
your mouth falls open to it
it renders you
tenders you
strips you
strokes you
kindles you
rides you
screams you
cleans you
clears you
sings you
buries you
kills you
births you

hands you back to yourself
sometimes swaddled
with warm mother's two hands

a kiss to your forehead
you emerge damp and wrinkled
yet promised well

or it might dump you on the doorstep
of your forgotten memory
a foreign land
leaving you hanging
incomplete
wanting more
or much less

however you come out
you are changed
a chink shifts
a lever falls into unparalleled
positional space
unvisited

your scripts are
exchanged
your boughs and wings
made new

you dock gently
bumping up toward
surface's edge
your keel scraping softly
as you rise
and breach topside

your mouth opens
once more
this time to release
a velvet sigh

and life's stage curtains
breathed closed by breath

raise
for your reentrance

THE PRICE

One.

the mistranslation
of one look can cost you
your youth
maidenhood
and every one of your
young woman's dreams

ripe wheat
reaped
gone
the years passed
without feeling
them go
never checking the mail

persephone's road
to the underworld paved
with no mother looking
demeter goes the other way
spring freezes over
deaf to daughter's cry
as hades covers her mouth
and pulls her under

I thought when you found us
that time
on the couch
in a house we ought not have

been inside of
his one hand on my naked
breast
his other hand
god knows where

our eyes met for the length
of the rest of my life
and I saw your lips furrow
pucker
purse
your eyebrows
V together
the huff
from your mouth
soiled me
and the turning
of your body
from the sight
froze the crystal
of my body

I was indigestible

left behind
an appetizer gone cold
tossed into the bin
during cleanup
without a thought
for how it came to be
assembled
in just that way
worthy only of the trash
put out on regular
wednesdays

meant for savoring

and slow chewing
with an mmm escaping
as the swallow comes

just not meant for him
the gourmet dinner he stole
that you left on the table

I was not meant for him

the scowl
I saw there
flash burned my body
scarring it
braising it blackened
like the time I was sat
on the stove at two
the burner lines
still arc on my left calf
it was
an accident

all the long moments
contained within the border
of a year
two
ten
twenty
thirty
still scald
spoiling goods

my spring
turned to winter
in that moment
of hurricane
demeter turns away

from persephone's cry
the pomegranate gone rotten

Two.

here I am at forty-nine
back on that couch
in my mind
the memory reel on repeat
I see something
I never saw before

your leaving remains
in frame
but demeter's reason
is not what I thought
it was

she was ice bound
with the storm
galing in his face
her heart gripped
inside an iron fist
the one ripping
open my fruit
in the wrong season
out of order
the whites of her eyes
tell the true story

when I slow the film
and stare from this perspective
pan in

I see not disgust
but horror

cementing for me now
how I missed this meaning
my translation was wrong

the result of the leaving
still the same
but it wasn't hand-me-down trash
she saw in me

what I saw her see
was me her daughter persephone
being devoured by hours
in the wrong phase
on phony stage
losing her body's country

and she the mother at arms
the demeter who'd left her post

I was her daughter
but I might have been herself

HOMAGE TO MY HEARTBREAK

when I kneel down before you
and open your edges
I become the wave inside your ocean deep
inexplicably
drawn toward your body line
I rush upon your shore and pour
into the lap of your soul
all aching arms and body burning on fire

      I
         break
              over
                    you

drowning inside of your wet mouth
full of moon at midnight
you saturate me
and like breath in the wind
you disappear
into the pull of my hawk eyed suns

EMPTY CHAIR⁺

a way to access those parts
you banished
you burned
you hated
you left on the side of the road
you strangled

took their voice and
for extra measure
buried it underneath
the horse you just dug
its grave for
assurance you will not
resurrect it
you wouldn't dare dig up those
sacred bones

is an invitation
a beacon
a sign of completion
a remembrance
a vacancy
an availability

a chance

a place of honor
a beckoning
a potential
where you claim the present

and requiem the past
stay put
where you integrate
all the abandoned selves
of you

a way to hear them
scream
whisper
plead

for your return

for your reclamation
of all of you

a place to rest

to take witness

of your willingness

a hand reaches back
from the future to come
out from the kaleidoscope
of infinite to-comes

to invite you to step up
step forward
step out step in

your future sings at the gate
the code to enter
has been on your arm all along
an unseen tattoo

bring your arm to your forehead

your hand to your cheek
breathe in
then out

open your grave-risen mouth
the notes lift out of cells
bubbles you catch on your tongue
to feel the initiation song

swallow and take yourself in
a communion of your own life liquid

then blow
blow gently

and a dandelion imprinted
with your calibration
floats out of your mouth
and
you hear your own song
and call yourself

a golden lasso
encircles your wrists
guides you to the chair

a prisoner to joy
you speak only truth
your own
proclaim yourself
your own agent
of belonging

wishing nothing more than
to invite those yet unlassoed

who have not heard their own music
come sit in this empty
chair

it waits for you
as it once waited for me
where I laid beside it
and proclaimed the
abusers done with me

then climbed back to my feet
unstable and wobbly
unused for decades

and took to my throne
where we all can sit to feel
our completion

of this piece
of this moment
of wishing for the sharp edge
to claim the red life
out of our arm
distinct from the gate code
the entryway to our lives

no
we no longer
wish to harm

but to restore

the harmed becomes the healer

I rise

from the chair
leave it empty
still warm

it waits for the next woman
for you?

it is a garland of olives
the branches will hold
come sit

HERD MEDICINE

Dear Cicero,

You were in my life only a short time, but you—dapple grey off-the-track Thoroughbred with flaxen mane and tail, black stockings, and impossibly high withers—requested something different of me than all the others. As your name implies, Cicero, you did not beat around the bush in your communication. You were not subtle and made each meaning clear.

I called you Cicero Skywalker because riding you was like floating with the clouds; you were so tall and smooth. You were a delightful wonder under saddle. But when I was on the ground, you only talked about two things. One was you didn't like to be groomed or touched much at all, and the other was you needed more room to move. I thought how this kind of sounded like me. I dismissed it. I wouldn't believe or listen to a horse saying you didn't want to be touched by me. And I thought surely you could simply adjust to the amount of real estate I had to give.

Our grooming sessions were the worst. I'd give you a firm sweep with the body brush and you'd flick and swish your tail at me. I'd try a soft bristle brush and you'd pin your ears. I'd try a curry comb and go in gentle circles, loosening dirt and hair, and you'd lift a hind leg all the way up and kick straight out. Many times narrowly missing an unsuspecting dog going by, minding her own business.

At this point, you were screaming at me with your body to stop touching you. It's true that some Thoroughbreds are superfine skinned and ticklish to groom. But this went way beyond that, didn't it? I didn't want to hear you. I wanted to have the joy I got from grooming horses. Except it was never a joy, because you hated it. You would only accept my bare hand sweeping off where the saddle would go, and then only sometimes. We'd go round and round like this until I just stopped. Your body language was undeniable.

I arranged the movable corral pieces and pastures in such a way that you had the most room on the property. Though you were an ex-racehorse, you didn't often run. Instead, you patrolled the fence lines, scanning the horizon. Even though I'd look where you were looking, to illustrate that I was listening to your concerns, I could never relieve your burden. You took to kicking the barn, both from the inside and on the outside, and you wouldn't stop. I had to admit it, you weren't happy and desperately wanted me to hear you. I surrendered, listened, and acknowledged what I heard you speaking.

It was up to me to help you. And I did. I found you a home with a gal who had forty acres and no barn but a perfectly nice run-in shed. The day she picked you up, I was sad to see the beautiful and dignified animal you were leave, but knew I was making life right for you and that I got you where you needed to go. In the trailer, you put your long head against my chest for a full minute. I wiped my eyes and put my face into your mane. *Thank you, dear Cicero, for teaching me to listen when it's sometimes the hardest thing to hear.*

I closed the trailer ramp and turned to your new owner. I handed her an old and worn, but soft cloth covered in grey hair. "Here, this is what he likes."

Thank you.

All my love,

Christin

A THOUSAND TONGUES⁺

sing showers of blessing
hope is restored

we lose sight
of gloom

resurrection child
turn around to break down
death

peace
be still in your doubt
receive glory

turtledoves utter justice
truth is found
in the street

morning has broken
many troubles
you are safe

my heart teaches
presence

let love show me
the path to life
fill me with enduring joy

may the spirit
in the evening
lock the fear temple
breathe and receive
the holy dream

offer praise
to the source power
kingdom
come
deliver evil

break the cup
come as you are

pray mystery

alleluia

BASIC INSTINCT

your presence
a domino of hide and seek
I strain to frame into reason
what can it possibly mean
beyond the addition of chromosomes
and a roof over my head

harkened human basket
each one of us carries
and fills over the course of our lives
collecting each piece and bit
minor and profound
wisdom both apparent and arcane

mine lined with bronze gauze
of mind dream and patchwork plans
sacred cloth to cut
an outline of an offering
a basin for you to fill
tattoo the blank stone of my heart
where I wished you could inhabit
and write your name

dad

I journal
the same entry over many years
when I have wanted to die
what stayed my hand?
I look into the basket

and pull out something
I had not noticed before
I walk all the way around it
open my palm as if I could
hold it in my hand

your desire to breathe
and to stay alive
when your chest
ratchets your ribs
into steel cables that do not move

is the inspiration
and expiration
that opens my eyes
and flowers me

you cling to nature's law
of existence and survival
claw
crawl
away from the spur
of death

I witness you father
bargain for breath
rolling dice with your
smoke-filled whittled lungs

a gill carved from regret

your offerings of caffeine
alcohol and nicotine
brought before the altar
of your heart
that your yellow hello fingers present
are the alms of highest value

its broken beat swollen
with the bounty of short supply

no myrrh nor frankincense
the wise man did not come
your mother not fully loving
your image
a cracked vision and
the shadow of imperfection

so instead surgically altered
your appearance
when you were seven
her name was not mary
today underneath
greying ringlets
and your smoking halo
the fire-tipped white wand
billows poison fog
I find you father

clasping the porch railing
where you must lean
to stand
your spine bowing
to unseen gods nearby
waiting with their golden nets
in case your body
rejects itself for the final sacrifice

I watch you fight to stay
on this blue pearl
finite home

where contracts cash out
to send us back through origin's tunnels
to the place beyond the last drop

of ocean
the last electron of space
beyond the coffee dregs
you study the bottom of your cup
instead of me

where the rainbow has not yet
entered onto the loom of itself
still gathering thread to spool
color banner choices yet to be cast

I watch you strain
to stray
far from your memory

stretching across your brain-bridge
to mine the life left
trickling underneath
honeycombed in beer cans and butts

sour grounds can't tarnish and fade
your ability to wonder at the sky
or your grown children's faces
or their children
but
your only need and focus
is to stay

somehow stay

the gift exchange railing thin
I watch you
trash your greatest jewel
the body you came here in

with each puff and sip
the coughing coming up
from your smoldering soul
exhausting you alive

what I learned from you father
is my ordinary treasure
that's rested and waiting
in my basket
of life's best prizes
unrecognized until now

the shape of staying

what I learned from you father
is how to stay when I wanted to die
the blueprint we share
indexes our time capsule

that you seal with a kiss
that rare moment you rise
out of the bog to walk on water
in my eyes

lips to my forehead
though you struggle to move
with your first and final partner
the blessing of your breath

later
when I can
come to thank you
for what I have found

daddy you whisper
your beloved voice a rasp
against my ear

that's alright baby
that's alright

MOTHER, WHO WE HAVE BECOME⁺

is not who we once were
in the time of before

we have both changed
in the time since I told you
in the time since I told you

there has been silence
long long silence
where we each drowned
in the truth of what happened
and the role we each portrayed

you the protector
who did not
me the victim
who was

to my surprise the cord has grown
stronger
despite the fraying
the unraveling
rewinding and reweaving of itself
with each passed night
of sorrow
each repentance
each hail mary mother of god
each day of life
alive with the sorry scars
re-scratched to bleed

there had to be hell
had to be hell
where each one of us tarried and carried
then unpacked the black-holed bag
of shame cold loss and grief
with no other choice
but to face
what had been placed
on the table

now unpacked and laid out
ready to be remembered
laundered and tendered

sticks and stones make broken bones
you washed what you could
made your best attempts
to mend
the torn knees you found
with fresh needle and thread
both of us resisting the eye
but the force of that force
that blows tornados and breathes the fish
and flies the birds
and blooms roses
undulates chests and thunders hooves

kneads the bread of life
and pulled us through
this unfenced vacuum
our glaze
kiln bronzed pushed close
to shattering

you scrub clean the thighs
with the hottest water and soapiest lye

both yours and mine
we have become raw
raked with all of it

outrage and anger
staining us
no matter how much we swab and scour

How could this be
It wasn't me
It didn't happen
I wasn't there

we both cry the same story
each experience turns
only a slight degree of revolution
different from the other

as the dawn must follow night
we must fall again into
orbit with each other

the umbilical
a channel we both pass through
bidirectional

who is mother
who is daughter

there is no telling
anymore
your mother abandoned you
her mother abandoned her
and you have abandoned me
all the same
for different reasons

some justified some not
yet
still

now we cycle back together
encircling our horses beloved
and they encircling us
nose to tail and tail to nose
closing out time
relinquishing space

a horse stands in a pasture alone
her gold mane lightly billowing
this early sentient jewel
we each belong to most
talisman
herd mender
gate watcher and heart code keeper

we walk in this field
from opposite directions
our hands out gliding over tall wintered grass
a world in between us shimmering
I approach her east
you approach her west
our arms outstretched
in offering to her
she turns her regal head
to accept your west and then my east

our palms open up toward
the mountain of her miraging body
fans of finger tendons
skyward lift

we touch her finespun coat of pearling moon
caress her momentarily

our hands pass through her soma
her hologram of heaven
our palm-soles cradle and cup
this soul mare's heartbeat chalice
we drink across this altar
in spirit's synchrony to find
our polared hearts aflamed alive
in alchemy

the goddess mother mare dissolves inside us
our hands join and fingers interlace
the silver queen high above
winks her open eye
flashing mercy's face
lighting up our pardon
lighting up our pardon

we remain standing
on our four feet
and thrown wide open
and unbroken
the barn doors of our hearts
rubedo red repaired

THE PEONY KEY⁺

Traveling weaver genuflect
when stillness rides the lightning

Wake up now
go into the diamond
lap the crystals at its water's edge

Together we crafted
this plan for you
then ordain you forget
so you could remember
after the scorching of your spirit

We will call you
to uneat your tail
drag it through blood
and paint your cheeks
you will finally
recognize yourself

The initiation will be a razor
to your breast
which you will not feel
but welcome

Rescue the children
they will find you
they are coming
from every direction

their muzzles bless you
to do our work

Your candle gives
a great light
we see the fire
on your cheeks
you will step into the flame
we set for you alone

You have studied yourself hard
and we honor your cost

It was composed in carbon
and astral blood
you approved it
then stepped through
and forgot

Now it is time to remember
the wind is in your mouth
we taste you

Your peony is ready to be kissed
we are ripening you
one bloom at a time

We never forsake you
we were raped with you
we felt you disappear
that was how you said it would be

You stun us with your bouquet
its glory was unexpected

Pull up a bit
and let the horses
color your hair with gold
you are your own savioress
we will teach you how
be ready
rise now and sing
the song we named you

Your bones have shattered
their splinters lodged within us
we will return them one by one
you will hand them out
to those that need you

You have always been enough
suicide does not become you
we took that away
the laying of peonies and roses
at your feet on a bier
that loss
your world would not bear under

We will lullaby you
to sleep each night
pierce you again and again
you cannot help but be riddled
do not patch the holes
we will lick them
keep them clean
and you will find your courage in them

You will have all the time back
that was taken and lost
at the mark of half your life

One day soon you will look
at the past you bore
begin to smile
then laugh without ever
stopping

Pluck us like peaches
that we may drip off your chin
we lodge in you our arrows
these are the answers
to your questions
use our tips
we will scribe for you
electrify your prayers
follow the crumbs atomic

Surrender back into your life
you will go through the portal
wearing the stars in your hair
blinking the night
from the grasp of day

Ravage your life to its death
use it completely until nothing remains
you have been seasoned enough

Our teeth stamp you
we have skipped nothing with you
we keep the match to your flame

You will never go out
you are the candle
you are the original pattern
you are the miracle we made
for this moment

Your time has come light rider
torches will pass to you

Retrieve your spirit
a wildfire that runs unchecked
yet harms none

We shrouded you as long as we could
and can no longer restrain the brilliance
we shield our eyes from you
the entire length of your life
the night you do leave with us
the sky will black out
but not yet

We will fly kites that only you can see
from them we will hang the keys
that will only fit in you
you will be struck
by our lightning
when you grasp them
illuminate yourself

Don't mistake the dew in our eyes
for it's pride we have in you
we like how you worship
at our buffet
placing every letter
we have ever sent
every crystal bone feather shell snakeskin
seed pod tooth and holy grail
on your altar

Lengthen your stride now
breathe in the amnion
and read the oracle
that is your own body

your longings will not be left
unanswered

We love you without end or beginning
even as one by one the petals fall

ROAD MAP

first you allow your heart to break
then you dip your face in cold water five times
you sigh

you emerge out of denial
and walk the block with your dog
then you sing or hum or chant a mantra song

you put blame where it's meant to go
on the chests of those that hurt you
then you look up and forgive yourself

you come to your senses and ask what do I see smell hear
you taste
you touch

find the way to metabolize your shame
scribble and journal
drive to barnes and noble
then your favorite green space

you put your back up to a tree
you practice
inside I am aware of
outside I am aware of

count exhales for one minute
count down your breath from ten to one
regulate your autonomic nervous system

slow down
zoom out
notice and name

face your fears and flashbacks one by one
do downward dog for five minutes
butterfly tap your breasts with breath

you turn toward your triggers and hold out your hand
write an acrostic
go on a glimmer hunt and quest for awe

you fully feel and safely express your anger
you are witnessed and held by people
who care
know
and understand

establish internal safety
identify clues and cues
that welcome and warn
reach out and make contact

you look and feel
you recognize your place in the world
you locate your belonging
you walk on the beach pick up shells

reclaim your self agency and authority
scream keen and cry
sit and lie on the ground

even if you crawl
you find your way
to other survivors
and look into their eyes
see you aren't alone

you make the bed
put the kettle on for a cup of tea
pit the avocados and scramble the eggs

you take back your pleasure and find your joy
run the hottest bath
add essential oils and salt
smell steam read dream

you do angel wing and bee breaths
the vagal reset
you swim
you shower

you heal your body at the location of the harm
lie down and rock your body with your feet
do twenty jumping jacks in the kitchen

you find a new recipe
you shop for it
you make it

do the dishes
come out of isolation
enter community

pet the dog
groom the horse
clean the stalls

you find your way to post traumatic growth
find acceptance
understand your scars become sacred

make coherent new meanings
rewrite the narrative
listen to music

rearrange the dolls
furniture
cut your hair

you claim the gifts
scattered behind by the wreck
unwrap resilience
creativity flexibility and empathy

you gaze in the mirror
you made it
you claim compassion

you dance to one song
make the voo err ahh
sound mmm or omm

you practice the vagal break
inhale open my hand
exhale close my hand

groom yourself
to your own liking

eat pavlova with strawberry
pomegranate and passion
fruit and cream

YOU LIVE.

AMOR FATI

the final turning
is more than rote acceptance
it spins beyond the sight of the sun
rising and setting
and all that occurs between
in the flash of our decades

there is ever a crossroads
and the decision to cross
the threshold or not
is ours

when we stride along our shoreline
body line
fence line
the edges of ourselves

we cannot tell the pattern
we came here to fulfill

we must zoom out to view
and focus our fresh-found country
that lights the candle
of our being
and includes the punctuation
of the call we hear to heal
an exclamation

to incarnate the daimon
the shape that molds our soul

is to claim our genesis
our one devotion
that causes the labor pain
of its birth and bloom
to be rapture in sane

after the trespassing of our body
the tearing of our soul fabric
reveals torn away places
empty holes
sections of stitches ripped out

we can fashion something new
and what I do
with what's been left
is my choice to take

the time to say yes
to the rest of my life
is now
the time to let life rush in
is now

I do not like what has happened
to this body of mine
but I love what I've become
and I entrust myself to fall in love
with my life
my ability
being
and belonging

my body is mine
and you cannot have it
unless you have been
invited

I kneel before my colors
placed on the altar for me
I pick them up
in two hands
and I will saturate my stencil
in and out of the lines
in every way I'm called

survival is real
recovery and return to life
can happen
it's our choice
to leave it or to take it

in the magic of one moment
when garnet-breasted robin
landed in front of me
on the road one late
and dappled afternoon
under forested sun of a vision fast

where I was knighted Radiance

to stare at me and say

be only like me
for I am only myself
and you are only yours

I knelt
and snapped awake
rode my psyche headlong hard
into a rose and silver tornado
to sever antiqued matrix outworn
the wisdom answer found self described
inside the acorn

this paradigm pivot
offers me up my broken cup
glued back to whole with gold
filled with my philosophy stone
brew I bring it to my lips

and as the liquid descends
both cool and warm combined
laced with spice honey berry
leather lace myrrh and ginger
my kukeon elixir

I open my arms
and welcome home
my fate

and as I embrace her
the gift I offer to honor
her purpose and the hood blood
she did collect to provide
back to me
I cradle
in one outstretched hand
this book
to lay at the feet
of my first won beloved
new borne discovered
myself

I hemorrhage in love
with my own fate
we dance
in holy step

I sacredly surrender
my resistance to being alive
to a grave

it is not yet time to
occupy

I thrum with the hum
of my new found faith
following this life review
I brand my visible and indivisible
attitude
an invocation billboard
in fountain-penned tattoo
beneath a vein that follows
a rebuilt fence line from the
extension of my heart
past
the down-soft side of my left arm
on out

amor fati

and proclaim myself
to myself

f i n a l l y
home
come

ELEGY

if I hadn't been a survivor
I would have been a scholar

but perhaps a scholar after all
a student of myself

to learn to piece together
with my own sinew

what was scattered
and dispersed

quilted into wholeness
a one-of-billions human work of art

the story told along the lines
each stitch a blown out star

taking what was banished
back forward to the start

to unwrap the minted present
of this shiny new embroidered stole

to wear across the shoulders
and step into rightful reign as woman

personal queen of grace's night
in service to each day

and every woman who has ached
over her half-lost life

to the scholarship of survivors
I bow

WHO AM I

to write this book
for I'm not fully healed
not to call myself recovered
like done completely
and in a tense we recognize as past

you might be dropping
down your cup
liquid sloshing over

"wait a minute
I've been spending all this time
reading to discover
how I maybe might myself
reach the other side of harm
and here you say
you're yet the pilgrim?"

I'm ashamed
I find myself with a rust-bound anchor
around my neck
and diurnal drowning
my reminder every day
as prometheus endured the eagle
of all occasions and cases
it seems I've failed
to be mended

with no right to hold
this excalibur

they call the pencil
white knuckles glowing
against the gold
to record the kinds of losses
not only those I've had
but ones imagined I keep having

I sink
stuck as artax
in the bog of sadness
in the neverending story
rotten garbaged murk
sucks on the hooves of my feet
its lush loam swells to pour
into my nostrils
I am exhausted in my eager
for a final rendered exit

in my last imagined seconds
I wail questions with no sound
from the empty tomb
of my mouth

what have I really overcome
who am I to write this?
what have I accomplished
that could count
toward this embrazened rescue
the reassertion of myself
and to be writing this all down?

I can conjure nothing
and drop my graphite cutlass
in defeat

I free fall
with no remembrance for the parachute

my star child self
hand packed inside my heart
my celestial wind suit
shivs open cerebellum spasms
the fresh-formed daily scabs
covering my sores
slash open raw once more

until I remember the ripcord
and feel brave enough to pull
which sends a diving valentine
to retrieve me
as I plummet
I am prized
up and avert sure collision
with the earth

and in the twilight out from mars
I begin to witness
in a hypnogogic dream
my own amendment
a parade of floats appears
each one a broadcast play
of every stride I've taken
every scene of reclamation

a self-conducted orchestra
of steps appraised and taken
even faced the face of death
I endure the desiccation
suffer through denialing
wide open deserts
turning burning into baptism
its cleansing terminality
hollow me empty

so ecstasy can but soon

be welcomed galloping in
a grand prix test of the goddess rites
to vanquish back the stolen land
the self-booned riches
of my worth

in a flash I saw myself
set within a star
and I could view that astral self
as if I were astride
each angle of the points
all five and forever
beaming out and also looking in
this is what I saw

the way a life is a mantle
woven on skeletoned loom
and placed on human scaffold
each occurrence names a color
tile ribbon twine or texture
a bitter and nectar papyrus
read with fingers and felt with eyes
draped or flown
a cloak couture designed
with only me in mind

I'm hailed to whoa by cosmic thumb
every single item
on my restoration road map
I have put a check by
thresholds I have crossed back over
all the territories I retook
tucked safe inside orion's belt
strung across my hips with heart
slung way low and sexy

gospel thrums

the kernel of my bosom
I grant
I have failed but once!
and that's to see the number
of reset stars rehung
igniting burning bold
they dazzle on my tongue

the ribbons roll out my rainbow
across my limber crust
my life claimed back by me
a rosette shimmery
of first place cerulean
pinned inside my shoulder
for only me to know

all the years blown out
have not been idle frippery
I have ridden out
from the bog my blade
held high in both my hands
bloodstained forearms to the elbows
address the battles I have won
my body doing sanguinary labor
in the underground inferno
scalded scarred and maimed
my purple hammered heart herculean strong
and yet waving is the banner
that bore my life reborn
I have not been doing nothing
I got myself to here
this is what I see
and this
is everything

then the small voice whispers
there's one more notch

to be pinked
one last jewel to affix
to cassiopeia's crown
years marched by while I was warring
I said "not-that, not *that* now!"
and oh I know *not-that*
is now
my cherried resurrection

but how do I go there
to that place I've never trekked
who will point to that direction
who can guide me how

the answer avalanches
out from the ground
erupts the answer of itself
across my face
it's you

and in that evanescent instant
I know that I possess the course
and how
and that I'm the only one
it's true
no technique to study
no book or cherished counsel
no future waiting room of time
will be the thread to twist to twirl or twine

this last instruction appears as bread
fresh baked toasty warm
and wholesome
with yeast aroma to nourish me
this is what to do
to get home
the manna you must eat

take my hand in mine each part
and one by one invite each fear and shame
enter into private interview
to settle their scares and scores
we sit on our conjoined heels
from our knees we bow
our foreheads touch together
our hands pressed down
upon our patchwork quilt in progress
spread out across the grass and sky
to ratify our meeting
the unburdening will start
its weaving spindle bobbing
easing skeins for dreams
through our veins
to find the portals out

from a goodie basket near my side
I'll offer seltzer with hearty sandwiches
bites of chocolate cake and berries
fears can air themselves and refresh
shames can spin their cyclones
off from sticky fingers
I'll take their notes
and hear them out completely
promise all the time to take
to show and tell their needs
no matter their requirement
I'll not move
from my station
their legacy will be repaid
their transmutation made

I've avoided them too long
forcing magic that they would stop
pounding on my door for justice
if only I kept looking out the window

or killing all spiders spinning
the webs that nerved their screaming
through my hallowed bones

each concern will take
a ticket with a puncture
embroidered with offenses
too terrible to name
clock out only when and not before
the tapestry on loom
can come to shred
this stale story
and recycle dream-yarn to refashion
pristine regalia to include
what's been inexpressible
and un-approached

if read from left to right
my barren cache of parchment
this final band of ribbon
this spectrum of myself
is singed with nothing scribed
my last frontier untouched

to my aphrodite
her queendom a charnel ground so burned
this last task I will prove
as paid the forecast of her holy ransom

I am now become the venus
rising from deep blue
scallop shell be damned
instead I borrow cupid's arm and bow
and from my female fallow quiver
aim my incandescent arrow
to berth a bullseye
into my sacred spouse

and by my choice built of brave and brazen
be yoked in night-clad rhapsody
and open beguiling oyster blush
my long due salt and honey

then morning after harmony
sit to write
my scrivener's song of paradise
across this barren landscape
that was before my body

and so when of myself I ask
who am I
and with what authority
to write this book
held in your hands
one not fully holy healed
just yet but riveting
the fracture closed and fast
as comets streaking dakini dust
behind my horses' chariot
our lungs on fire
lunging for the wire
and the roses
for my *life* to win

who am I
to write this book

I sing

who am I
to *not* to

I am not what happened to me, I am what I choose to become.

—based on the collected works of Carl Gustav Jung

EPILOGUE

At the point in life when we are ready to choose to take responsibility for ourselves, our actions, and the course of our lives, and begin a journey of healing from any hurt or harm we have encountered, even from simply being a human, we open a door, previously closed, to potential and possibility. Suddenly, all things become imaginable. Even those we never thought plausible. Sometimes, especially those.

In safe and healthy relationships, ruptures are more likely to be noticed and named. Which in turn may lead to repairs offered and, in time, a return to relationship is enjoyed and may, in fact, be strengthened. These are healthy expressions within relationships ranging from friends and family to intimate partners to coworkers, bosses, and even between therapists and clients.

When healing from childhood sexual trauma, the likelihood of a repair from the outside in any form is almost always zero, unless there is justice served by the legal system. Which is not often the case, and certainly wasn't in mine. This invites the burden of repair to come from within the one whose body has been crossed. This is a difficult endeavor and can feel monumental to approach, especially as a survivor. The task of how to offer oneself the reparation and repair, to reclaim the temple of our body, is a primary and necessary piece of healing that will never come from the perpetrators.

It is a painful enterprise I have enacted and embodied. Though it has taken decades, I have made these repairs to myself. There were unexpected gifts along the way that I harvested with awe and gratitude, which I deposited into a basket like sweet carnelian McIntosh apples, these diamond shards of wisdom.

And yet, there was still more for me to discover and experience. As there always is. For healing, as living, is a spiral. And more always comes around.

One month prior to my scheduled printing date, I received a break-of-dawn, morning email. It was from one of the men who'd crossed my body, as a child, so many times, so many years ago. I nearly stopped breathing when I saw his name and went ice cold. Now, of all times. What could it be? Grown and mostly healed, I did not rush to click it open. I waited to set my perimeter in place. I took a shower. Got dressed. I walked my girl, Lali. I saw a new client and gave my full attention. Even attended a prescheduled online lunchtime workshop on boundaries. I ate my lunch. I journaled.

Then, finally, I sat outside, under my backyard tree, my hens content to scratch their yard earth, and as they quietly clucked their hymns, I called in my angels, ancestors, guides, and protectors, thought about the horses, took a breath, and read it.

It was an apology.

Thirty-two years later. Unbelievable. Some might even call it a miracle. I did. And then I was offered the fire quartz of grace.

Later that afternoon, I needed to lie down and rest. The day had been almost too much to take in. I lay down and fell quickly into a deep tunnel of sleep. And I dreamed a benediction.

I journeyed through a channel that cut through the darkness of my past and placed me solidly in a field in the present. A meadow of sweetgrass, with bronze, yellow, and rusted-henna-red wildflowers, pointed to a life approaching autumn. I looked around and twirled with my arms open. I saw the ruptures crisscrossing my body, the sutures standing out in the

EPILOGUE

relief of the gold glue of repair. The alchemy of skin and gold, pretty now and certainly beloved.

I heard the stampede of hooves through my bare feet and leg bones. The vibration opened my eyes, and I became aware of my heart-horse thundering his way toward me, parting the sea of grass and pressing the flowers to the earth. It was Wren. He slowed to prance himself to the edge of my toes, stopped, and placed his head next to mine. A pair of salt seas gushed from my eyes, and my heart became a buoy bobbing between them. I bowed and he spoke to me.

"I come now to let you know that I have never left you. You never treated me as property. You and I were one another's breath. From the moment I lay down to die with your arms around me, and my spirit split from the body that you knew, liberated from the lungs that contained your grief un-keened, I have flown beside you. I know that today you have heard from him. Dissolve him as a trigger, a drop of salt in water, and consider him, and them, no more. I emancipate you! I have come today to re member you to my presence and that you have never been alone. I have been here and will stay beside you. Inside your heart, I'll always be. Wake up now, Light Rider, and receive the blessing of my benediction from upon my brother's back. Bucephalus is coming for you and you will know him when the night before, in a dream, he will place his midnight velvet brow to yours, and a diamond will shine between your eyes!"

With a start, I woke up with wet cheeks. My hands clasped in the sheets, twisted in mane, heart thumping. Dreams can heal. I was smiling. And I still am. Thank you, Wren. Thank you, dream maker of Spirit poetry. Thank you, gods and goddesses, all. Thank you, Fathergod of Mystery. Thank you, Divine Mothergoddess of Consciousness, Love, and Justice.

I press my palms, and bow. I will continue to move, and on. And maybe one day far from now, after my last exhale, I'll get to sprout halo, hooves, and wings.

Anything is possible.

POSTSCRIPT[†]

Dearest Reader,

Not long after this benediction dream, exactly on time for my fiftieth birthday as promised, I received the blessing. The dream of the dark horse with a shiny diamond pressing his brow to mine *came true*. And after his mighty mythic-midnight-velvet body stepped down out of the trailer, he stood stock still. I listened closely, for he whispered his name to me. Bucephalus Mars. Indeed he is out of this world and, like me, a warrior, not for war, but for the primal sake of love.

I continue to heal. Some folks have their North Star. I have Mars. Anything really is possible.

Love,

Light Rider and Mars

LETTER TO SURVIVORS

Dear Survivors, dear Warrior Queens,

This is for those of you who have been to that place where your *no* meant nothing.

This is also for you if you didn't know you had a *no* that was yours to give.

This is for those of you who have lived in that place where the fake smile was your attempt to appear "nicer" so that you might be hurt less. That place where you knew that no one was coming to help you, that place where you disappeared, went away, because what was happening in the moment was too awful to stay inside of.

What I understand now, being on this side of recovery, is that I had to do hard things to survive. To make it this far. To remain on the planet. To stay. I now know from experience that there is an innate intelligence embedded in every act, response, and reaction, of our mind, heart, and body.

Sometimes I had to be depressed and unreachable. Angry and full of rage. Projective. Suicidal. Resentful. I had to isolate myself from the world for my own protection. Make myself small and unseen. Be unsuccessful, because I had to be safe. I kept others at a distance. Locked them out. Denied their help. Dismissed myself as unworthy. Hated myself and everything I was. Until the day that I didn't. I did all of these things to remain alive.

LETTER TO SURVIVORS

The first step toward healing from child sexual abuse, or any abuse, is to admit it happened. That sounds simple, but it's not. Just like many people around us, sometimes we want to be in denial too, because it can feel easier not to know. So we doubt our own perceptions and feelings. And bury our memories. Our hearts atrophy.

Maybe it didn't really happen, or it didn't happen that way. I'm alive, aren't I? How bad could it have been? Maybe these thoughts, those feelings, this numbness, aren't about anything real. Maybe it's all in my head.

I am a survivor. I know this is true. Over the years, often it was hard to identify myself as a survivor because sometimes it didn't feel as if I had survived yet. But I am here. And so are you.

Child sexual abuse imprints us with complex trauma. This can sometimes include suicidal thoughts, persistent depression and anxiety, unprovoked anger or the torment of numb passivity, flashbacks, nightmares, and problems with emotional and physical intimacy and sexuality. And there are confusing symptoms, like migraines, throat clenching, stomach pain, gut issues, chronic fatigue, hair-trigger emotions or no emotions at all, insomnia, daytime sleeping, muscle aches, teeth grinding, apathy, and hypervigilance. PTSD symptoms have slithered behind me like the ouroboros, with the serpent eating its own tail. My tail. And always, the debilitating doubt and isolation. At times it feels like a one-way ticket to hell.

Stepping onto the path of recovery and healing takes courage. Recovery touches every surface of harm and crisscrosses the landscape of a lifetime. The path is never a straight line. And you will be on that path both in solitude and in community. Even if it's just a community of one. A trusted therapist, a woman who has been there, or even a horse. Although usually it's a string of allies who might be with you for years or simply for one heart-opening moment. Each serves as a strong solitary post standing in a long, wandering line of way stations as you travel through this uncharted topography.

LETTER TO SURVIVORS

My own pilgrimage of healing and recovery from child sexual abuse inspires me to be part of your community. Survivors need other survivors. I am one of those fence posts, buried deep and solid in the ground, that can withstand the pushing, pulling, and thrashing that healing on this level demands. I want to be that voice that recognizes the pain and harm that has been done and gives you permission to heal. And the one who can hold you while you do it.

I want and aspire to be the voice that says *You have an intrinsic right to feel better. To enjoy life. To thrive rather than struggle to get by.* I want to be the voice that tells you that one day you will be able to look back over your shoulder and reflect, but not drown. You will be able to ride forward into your future without being imprisoned by the past. I want you to know what I have learned—that your healing path can bring you into an extraordinary realm that lies beyond mere surviving.

In this collection of memoir poetry, I introduce you to the metaphor of recovery as riding down a fence line and attending to the breaks that need to be repaired. Those sites are where the gloom leaks out and the light struggles to get in. Where the weeds grow. And I can tell you that the repairs you make will not match the original fence. It can never be as it was. Give yourself time to mourn that.

Ultimately, it's up to us what we do with our ripped and torn fences. Even if we choose to repair them or not. We each have our own timing. I did. It took me over thirty-five years to recognize the ruptures and name the destruction. To recognize that what happened actually happened to my own body. What is left unrecognized and unfelt has a funerary force of gravity that can swallow us into a black hole. In order to heal we must feel. And the deepest woundings often yield the deepest healing.

At times we might choose to allow some places to stand ragged and wrecked, a testament to what's been done to us. To those places especially, we can offer kindness, a promise to not forget what's happened, and a personal pledge to return once we are ready.

In our healing we can craft memorials, shrines, and altars and leave them at different locations along the terrain of our bodies or in selected places inside our homes or in nature. We might build rock cairns that represent the times we were able to visit a particular wounding but couldn't linger. The cairns can grow and change each time you visit. The process and ways of repair in which healing can happen are limitless and personal. As individual as you and me.

I recognize now the messages and signs my body posted along my boundary line. My body showed me those places of trespass that so badly needed my tending, the places where I'd lost my body's sovereignty. But back then, I was lost. These were signs I couldn't read. Messages that made no sense and had no apparent origin or connection. There was no one to point the way or show me *home* on my compass.

Today I read these messages with great clarity, respect, and gratitude. I am able to respond with loving kindness, to answer and tend to what my body needs. I know my path of healing will continue, but I am grateful to be where I am. Now I can listen and speak the language of my body. We are finally friends and partners.

On this path you may think about your unlived lives. What might have been if all this had not happened. I have spent years pining. Dreaming about the life I thought I was going to have, the one I thought I was meant to have. The one I thought I deserved to have. I wanted to annihilate my history. But through the course of my healing, what I came to know was that if I could magically take away my suffering, I'd also annihilate the woman I have become. And when I see my complicated beauty, as a quilt laid out in a meadow, and ask *Would I make that trade?* The answer is always no.

I am not only the harm that has happened to me. I am who I am both because of it and in spite of it. And this realization plants my feet firmly in my life now, to weave that life into what I want with *all* my history, not just selected parts and secrets.

What has survived is me. Is you. Us. I have reclaimed myself, my value, worth, and pleasure. I have arrived into the daily practice of listening to my body and checking on what I need, looking for glimmers, scavenger hunting for awe.

I lean on practices that nurture and nourish me: journaling, dancing, building altars, practicing yoga, nature walking, stargazing, beachcombing, collage, tending the roses, snipping herbs for pesto, tending my chickens and collecting their blue, cream, and brown eggs, petting my dog, riding, grooming and caring for my horses, and making poetry.

Some might think it's an easy thing to recognize and know what nourishes us, but for survivors of child sexual abuse it is a new learning. It takes looking for the places and the times we feel the most at ease, least anxious and afraid, which, in itself, is a new and unfamiliar state. We can and must begin to orient ourselves around these new posts.

Making this discovery for ourselves is, without question, one of the most important things we can do. The way I took refuge in horses, nature, seawater, chickens, stars, and dirt didn't register as haven until much later in my recovery. When we identify these sources and pathways that allow and invite personal liberty and the space to breathe, we open portals to remember ourselves and get a glimpse of home. But it takes time to get to know ourselves, to discern what feels just OK and what feels just right.

Self-care is not an indulgence; it is a necessity not only for healing but for life. Until we come to value our own worth, we are rarely able to offer ourselves the gift of this care, and we won't stop kicking down the barn.

Another twisted layer of complication emerges out of a gross misunderstanding. Women can also feel especially betrayed by their own bodies during the abuse and in abusive environments. Our animal body responds naturally to stimulation. These feelings of betrayal are understandable and also misplaced. Even if your body may have responded biologically to stimulation during abuse, it does not mean you were not harmed. It does not mean you wanted it. It does not mean you invited it. It does not mean you deserved it. We, women, have a responsibility to educate ourselves about our body's very normal, natural, brilliant, and individual biological functioning. Once we do, we may afford ourselves profound levels of self-compassion and self-understanding. Our therapists, whether male or female, if they are engaging in offering healing work within this realm, have the same responsibility. If it is evident they have not done their own healing work, do not walk but run to leave them behind.

For me, it all started around age thirteen and ended only after I turned twenty. There were multiple men and an entire cascade of transgressions and commissions from the adults around me. Not even teachers of mine who knew dared to tell, to whistleblow. Instead they looked the other way. No legal action was ever taken on my behalf. What we all must understand is that boundaries are crossed in so many ways, with so many levels and layers of complexity, both subtle and overt. Simply being human casts a sticky net of needs that we can all become entangled in. The ripple effects extend deep into the web of adulthood. Things become acceptable that would never be so, except for the remaking of what is healthy and OK. And so we must ask ourselves, when we offer consent as adults, what part of us is doing the consenting? Our survivor part, maybe not yet fully healed? The part of us needing to feel connected and accepted? The part of us needing security and stability? The part of us too tired to say no or *not now*?

It could be possible that *all* women enter into the realm of survivorhood, or at the least as an experiencer, and have borne a crossing of some kind on the continuum. Where do you land? It could have been *just* a look, *just* a lewd gesture, *just* a crass word, or *just* a careless touch. Here, we have to look at how we use the word *just* as a diminisher. To different degrees, women, from every avenue of life, are groomed to believe this kind of behavior, and beyond, is normal. We lose perspective. We disconnect from our bodies. Violation lurks everywhere and in unexpected places. We must not minimize these crossings and the vital truth living inside our bodies. We are all brushed by the dust of our cultures, it's true. But humankind is still trying to figure out what it means to be human, to be kind, and to be just. Maybe once we do, we will begin to honor the voice, body, and soul of both the human and the more-than-human world.

This is also true: Healing is always right on time. In time with the stars, clouds, rivers, oceans, bloomings and witherings, moonshine and sunshine, and the slow roll of the planet. Like riding a horse along that fence line, there is the moment we loosen our reins, we allow the sway of our hips in the saddle, give our horse her head and the freedom to take us home. She knows. Our body knows.

If you are an ally, a therapist, family member, or friend, I hope that this collection will help you understand more deeply what this kind of experience is like and what is required of you to offer the safety and space that will allow your loved one's stories to gently and honestly come out from hiding.

Consider again this truth: You are here today. That means the past has already happened. You have already made it through the worst. You are here. You survived. You *are* a survivor. And so much more. Please care for yourself.

Sister Survivor Goddess, we need you here.

Thank you for staying.

Love,

Christin

RESOURCES

If you are in need of community and support, consider reaching out to one of these resources. Not every resource will be right for every individual, but you deserve a healthy community that is committed to your healing and safety.

If you are in the United States, remember that you can dial **988 for the Suicide and Crisis Lifeline** anytime, day or night. The **National Sexual Assault Hotline** is at **800-656-HOPE (4673)**.

There are many online sources of support, and I have chosen to list two here.

RAINN—the Rape, Abuse, and Incest National Network—is a national anti–sexual violence organization. Visit them at www.rainn.org.

The nonprofit Saprea group offers an extensive variety of online resources, including an informative webinar and a four-day in-person retreat available to women survivors of child sexual abuse. Learn more at www.saprea.org.

BOOKS

Anchored by Deb Dana. Published by Sounds True, 2021.
The Body Keeps the Score by Bessel van der Kolk, MD. Published by Penguin Books, 2015.

Call of the Wild by Kimberly Ann Johnson. Published by Harper Wave, 2021.

Come as You Are by Emily Nagoski, PhD. Published by Simon and Schuster, 2021.

The Courage to Heal by Ellen Bass and Laura Davis. Published by William Morrow, fourth edition, 2008.

The Courage to Heal Workbook by Laura Davis. Published by William Morrow, 1990.

Dream Wise: Unlocking the Meaning of Your Dreams by Lisa Marchiano and Deborah Stuart with Joseph Lee. Published by Sounds True, 2024.

Living an Examined Life by James Hollis, PhD. Published by Sounds True, 2018.

No Bad Parts by Richard C. Schwartz, PhD. Published by Sounds True, 2021.

Self-Compassion by Kristin Neff, PhD. Published by William Morrow, 2015.

The Survivor's Guide to Sex by Staci Haines. Published by Cleis Press, 1999.

Women Who Run with the Wolves: Myths and Stories of the Wild Woman Archetype by Clarissa Pinkola Estés, PhD. Published by Ballantine Books, 1992.

Writing as a Way of Healing by Louise DeSalvo. Published by Beacon Press, 2000.

TEN QUICK RESCUE REMEDIES / SOS TOOL KIT

I have listed a variety of mindfulness practices for you to explore if you are feeling dysregulated and ungrounded and in need of some quick support. *Mindfulness* is a buzzword these days. We can keep it super simple and keep in mind that mindfulness basically means paying attention to the present moment. Experiment with all of these remedies to find which ones resonate with you. If you discover that one doesn't work for you now, circle back around to it another time. You may find that these various tools and techniques work for you at different times. You might even consider tracking which ones are effective and when.

All of these short practices can serve to open the door to bringing your body and mind back into regulation. Feel free to change them to your liking and make up your own.

1. FLOAT

This is an easy-to-remember, brief mindfulness practice. Sometimes what can feel most supportive when we aren't sure what to do next is to follow directions. Here is a simple and short step-by-step mini ritual you can explore anytime.

F eel
L isten
O pen
A ttend
T rust

Now, let's FLOAT. Go slowly through the steps, one by one.

FEEL what sensations you are feeling. Is your body tight, buzzy, heavy? Do you feel anxious, angry, or melancholy?

LISTEN to your body speaking and to what self-talk you are hearing about what's happening.

OPEN into yourself and accept all that you are experiencing; lean into the sensations and emotions versus pushing away.

ATTEND to what you need to do in this moment to bring in some ease. If you aren't sure what small action to take, you may refer to some of the following quick remedies as a starting point.

TRUST in yourself and what you have discovered in this pause.

These steps cultivate mindfulness and a sense of being in the present moment. When we can land ourselves gently into the current moment, we have a greater potential to respond and make choices that nourish us rather than keep us wrapped reactively inside of our swirl.

2. Make the Bed

There can be times when we don't know what to do with ourselves and feel powerless to accomplish anything in our day. The simple act of making your bed can feel surprisingly productive. It also sends the message to ourselves that we have gotten up and are no longer in it, which, on certain days, can itself feel like a big win. Be sure to fluff the pillows!

3. Add Water

Water is life-giving. We spent nine months immersed in amniotic fluid. Our bodies are 70 percent water. We need water. Try these and notice how you feel afterward:

- Drink a full glass of water.
- Splash your face five times with water.
- Prepare a large bowl with cold water and ice. Dunk your face and hold for twenty seconds.
- Take a hot shower or bath.
- Make your favorite cup of tea.
- Play in the rain.

4. Move

Getting ourselves moving can serve as a reset button for our nervous system. Try these options:

- Dance your heart out to one song. Do it like no one is watching!
- Do twenty jumping jacks.

- Get on your mat and practice yoga for ten minutes.
- Go for a walk around your neighborhood and look for what captures your attention.
- Shake! Shake your body for two minutes. Pause and harvest the sensations.
- Go swimming. Return your body, even temporarily, to its original oceanic world to receive relief and refreshment.

5. Orient

Taking notice of our surroundings when we get lost in our thoughts or begin to feel out of control can be a quick way to bring ourselves back into present time. The first thing to do is lift your eyes. Ask yourself, *Am I physically safe right now?* If no, take steps to bring yourself to safety. Next, look outside, notice what you see outside your window. Look up. What color is the sky? Take in the room where you are. Look at the objects in the room, and perhaps one will capture your attention. Look at it closely and, if possible, hold it in your hand to study its qualities. Turn your head, neck, and eyes gently as far as you comfortably can to each side and momentarily focus on one object before turning back to center. Turning the head, neck, and eyes in this way tones the vagus nerve, which is a nerve bundle that supports us to feel safe and socially connected.

Here's another simple orienting exercise you can try that I call Come to Your Senses:

Tune into your senses one by one and notice what you see, smell, hear, taste, and touch. Speak what you observe out loud to yourself.

6. Take Notice

This is another remedy that has easy-to-follow directions. Explore each step to get yourself to the other side of a challenging moment.

- Notice and name.
    Notice what you are feeling and name it. Example: *I feel tight and hot, I am angry.* Or *I notice I am barely breathing, I am anxious.* Or *I notice my stomach hurts, I am sad.*
- What do I need?
    By asking yourself this question, you are honoring yourself and your feelings and highlighting your willingness to move toward a gentle shift of state. What you need could be to call a friend, take a break and go for a walk outside, or take a twenty-minute nap.

7. Listen to Music

Take five or ten minutes to listen to your favorite music.

Listening to music is restorative to our nervous systems.

If you enjoy listening to music and are a bit techie, explore the idea of making a playlist for your feeling states. Three basic feeling-state lists to start with could be contented, at ease, and happy; angry, anxious, and stressed; and sad, depressed, and sorrowful. Play each list as needed to give yourself permission and support to feel what you feel. You can expand your lists as you need and even give them interesting titles.

8. Touch

This is a kind of self-touch practice we can do for ourselves to initiate self-compassion and self-soothing. Here are a few ideas to experiment with:

- Place a palm to your cheek.
- Cradle your face with both hands.
- Butterfly hug: Cross your forearms to hold your upper

arms and rhythmically tap gently. The bilateral movements can be deeply regulating.
- Stroke your forearm.
- Place your hand to your heart.

9. Pet Your Pet

And here we come to my beauty, my teacher, my dog, Lali. She came to me when I was still angry, struggling, and not fully onto my healing path yet. She brought me her needs and her fears. I became capable of listening to her distress and giving her the gentleness I was not able to give myself yet. I began to trust myself to provide a safe relationship, comfort, care, and healing to her, and then to my own self.

Our animals can offer us great solace. Lean in to connection with them. The act of petting and engaging with our warm furry companions releases the hormone oxytocin into our bloodstream. This hormone is calming and helps us to feel safe, secure, and connected. Reflect for a moment how it feels when in the close embrace of a trusted loved one or witnessing the caring of others. You can even get down on the floor with your animal and spend ten to twenty minutes petting him or her and viewing the world from their perspective. Invite yourself into this gentle and nourishing experience.

If you don't own an animal, consider visiting your local animal shelter. You might even choose to volunteer or foster an animal needing a temporary home. Who knows, you may even get chosen by a dog or cat that can't wait to come home with you.

Taking care of an animal has proven health benefits and can bring a sense of purpose to our lives.

10. Breathe

This element is even more important than water. We must breathe to live. Thankfully our bodies do a super job of breathing for us. However, sometimes, our state of being can interrupt healthy and nourishing breath. When we become aware and conscious of our breath, we can make adjustments. Here are a couple of super-simple ways to bring more attention and mindfulness to your breath.

- Count your exhales for one minute.
- Count your breaths down from ten to one. You could use this pattern: On the inhale, silently say *inhaling ten*; on the exhale, silently say *exhaling ten*; on the inhale, silently say *inhaling nine*; on the exhale, silently say *exhaling nine*; and continue until you reach one.
- Set a timer for five minutes, find a comfortable seat, and simply observe yourself breathing in and out. Notice when your mind wanders and, with tenderness, bring it back to your breathing.
- Sigh! Out loud is even better. Even though this activity isn't always culturally accepted, when we sigh, it is our body endeavoring to reset us and bring us back into regulation. You will notice when you sigh, it relieves tension and that the exhale is usually much longer than the inhale. This is a powerful signal to our nervous systems that all is well, or getting there. Make sighing a regular practice.

THE PRACTICE OF WRITING

Writing is an open invitation. It allows every experience. It has no rules or boundaries. There is no right or wrong. It gives us the ultimate permission to include everything with nothing left out. You can write down every single thing you feel, don't feel, see, don't see, know, don't know, want to know, understand, and misunderstand. You can grieve, rejoice, love, hate, or desire on the page. It makes room for the grandest dream to be proclaimed, down to the tiniest detail to be described.

And try poetry. Especially poetry. It wields power.

Dr. James Pennebaker, a professor of psychology from the University of Texas at Austin, was one of the first researchers doing work on the effects of writing for healing. He began studying expressive writing in the 1980s and found that short writing sessions over a number of days, as few as four, resulted in beneficial effects on physical and emotional health and well-being.

He also found that people who kept their experiences secret exhibited many more health problems than those who expressed themselves in some kind of writing. Isolation and loneliness can kill.

Humans are meaning makers. The practice of writing is therapeutic and can help us make sense of our traumas and heartbreaking life events. It can help us transform our pain, let go of the past, and empower us to create a new life moving forward.

Here are a few exercises to get your pen moving:

- Timed writing. Put fifteen minutes on your timer and write without stopping. If you get stuck, make a list for the grocery store or tomorrow's to-dos; just keep writing. You may find once you get through the daily things, you begin to enter richer territory.
- Small writing. If vast empty white space gives you the jeebies, choose something smaller to write on. Use sticky notes. One thought for each note. Write for ten minutes.
- Write a letter. To yourself or a part of yourself. Perhaps the young child or young woman of you. Write to a parent or family member. Write to an abuser. Say it all. Everything you ever wanted to say but could not. You won't send these letters, but can choose to keep them in a private place to refer to later and see how your feelings may have shifted.
- Express yourself in a rant. This exercise lets you riff on whatever needs to come out. Let it all loose. Anger is welcome. Let it rip! You can choose to burn it and sprinkle the ashes in the trash if that feels liberating to you.

- Create a gratitude list. This is an oldie but still a goodie.
- Listen. Throughout your day, listen to people speaking, the radio playing, the TV, what the junk mail is selling, your bank teller, your kids talking with each other, and scribble down the words and lines that stand out to you. When you have a moment, write out all those words and lines. Look at the piece of found-text writing you have created. What does it say to you?
- Record your dreams. Afterward, you might be inspired to draw, scribble, paint, or dance them.
- Write a myth or fairy tale. If you are feeling especially writerly, you can experiment with this exercise I use often. I use oracle cards, tarot cards, birthday cards, or playing cards. Any kind of cards will do. Draw three cards. Using these cards as prompts, write a myth or fairy tale about your own life. You can start with "Once upon a time."
- Make a poem. Here is a stunningly easy way to begin: Write your name vertically down the side of the page. One letter for each line. Now go back and write a word or fragment that begins with that letter. It can relate to you or be unrelated. Voilà, you have written an acrostic poem. You can use this technique with any word or phrase.
- Explore the offerings of writing teacher, author, and safe-community builder Laura Davis: lauradavis.net.

SOMATIC WORK

Recovery that is true and deep must move through the mind into the body and touch into the places where the harm happened. I believe it is necessary to incorporate somatic work along the fence line of the healing journey.

Soma comes from Greek origin and translates as "body." Somatic modalities are ways to companion our body and cultivate the body-mind connection to support us to move toward reclamation and wholeness. Some examples of somatic work:

- **Gestalt**—This modality focuses on the present-moment expressions of the client. Body sensations, stances and armor, gestures, and sounds are tracked by the practitioner to bring awareness to the client's hidden core emotions and beliefs. Gestaltists engage in creating spontaneous "experiments" revolving around deeply held beliefs and stories to bring their client's background into the foreground, where unfinished business can be safely completed.
- **IFS**—Internal Family Systems suggests that we all contain many aspects or parts that function just like a family might, except on the inside. These parts of us can become frozen in the past when trauma is experienced, and then become saddled with protective roles they aren't equipped to handle. IFS is a modality that works toward unburdening these parts to restore wholeness and harmony to our inner kaleidoscope.
- **Mindfulness**—Practices that cultivate awareness of the present moment.
- **Yoga**—Specifically therapeutic and trauma informed. Find a teacher who will listen to you.
- **Principle-Based Partner Yoga** (founded by Elysabeth Williamson)—This important work invites the discovery of how safe touch, within a context of partnering, can serve to nourish, inform, and support the healing of psychic and somatic wounds sustained from being in relationship.
- **Massage**—Take time to find a body worker who can be sensitive to your needs.
- **Grof and Holotropic Breathwork**—These group-setting somatic practices cultivate self-exploration and personal empowerment through the acceleration of the breath and provocative music. They tap into one's inner-healing

intelligence and its innate capacity to guide us toward transformation and integrative unity.
- **Somatic Experiencing**—This work prioritizes the concepts of pendulation and titration. Clients learn how to move back and forth between states of feeling charged and feeling calm around their traumas.
- **Hakomi**—In this method, not unlike Gestalt, our human body is viewed as a window to access unconscious materials from developmental experiences that have shaped a client's core memories, beliefs, and worldview. The principles followed in Hakomi are mindfulness, unity, organicity, mind-body integration, and nonviolence.
- **EMDR** (Eye Movement Desensitization and Reprocessing)—This modality approaches a traumatic memory through "bilateral stimulation" to change the way memories live and are stored in the brain.
- **Flash Technique**—Similar to EMDR but does not require the client to think of traumatic events in order to reconsolidate memories.
- **Ecstatic Dance and Contact Improvisation**—These forms of dance support the cultivation of relational safety, partnership, and collaboration within a group. With ecstatic dance, the music is powerful and pulsing and serves as a vehicle to welcome participants into an open invitation to move their bodies, within the boundaries of their own comfort level, either solo or in partnership. Contact improvisation dance focuses more on partnering with others using principles such as counterbalance and contact. In both dance offerings, trust is cultivated with oneself in the midst of others.
- **SoulCollage**—I have listed this form of collage work here because it invites the whole body and psyche to participate in its creation. While choosing, cutting, and arranging images into mini works of art that express one's inner consciousness, one is encouraged to pay attention and be guided by their body in these choices.
- **Dreamwork**—There are many ways to begin the

nocturnal self-discoveries of the wise unconscious. As I noted before, begin recording your dreams in a diary or journal. You may start to notice themes and patterns. Jungian analysts and Gestaltists can be excellent dreamwork practitioners.

You will notice I have listed a blend of psychotherapies and modalities for you to choose from. The best way to get started with any of these possibilities is to go to your computer and google what options are available in your area. For many of these practices and methods, online and virtual offerings are in abundance.

Start slowly and listen to your body drawing you in one direction or another. Stay curious.

THE HEALING POWER OF EQUINE THERAPY

I recovered my soul through the heart of a horse.

Horses have been *the* way of healing for me. From that first ride, to receiving my first pony on my fifth birthday, and all the way to my fiftieth birthday, I have been a devoted owner, lover, advocate, and caregiver of equines, my entire life. These animals have stood by me, carried me, tested me, called me out, asked more of me than I thought I had, shattered me, respected me, partnered with me, and healed me. Through all the fence wrecking, riding, and repairing, we have been together. I owe a debt to them that I will gladly and enjoyably spend the rest of my life repaying.

Horses are healers. Their presence is undeniable. We cannot help but take notice. They invite us to pay attention—to them, to the environment, to ourselves. The very feature of their size can be initially compelling. Then once they have our attention and we are feeling more open and intrigued, we can begin to tune in to what is between us. If we become interested and curious, those qualities alone often indicate that our state of being has started to shift in the direction of regulation and that mindfulness has begun. One aspect they bring to humans is their example and expertise of the present moment. Horses live in this moment alone. They do not project into the future and they do not linger in the past.

The opportunities for nourishment, integration, and healing literally ripple out of their skin to touch our hearts, souls, and wounded bodies. Standing next to a horse can catalyze a change that catapults us into a new perspective, realization, fullness of mind, or awakening about who we are, how we have come to be, and the narratives we have woven for our own self-understanding and survival. The energetic heart field of the horse is so powerful, it can increase the heart rate variability of the human heart. This rise can foster feelings of calm, increase emotional availability, lower cortisol levels, and contribute to the regulation and reshaping of our autonomic nervous system.

Horses can literally change the meaning we have assigned to our stories and allow a new story to emerge.

In equine therapy, horses are co-facilitators and can offer as much direction and guidance as the practitioner. At times, even more. Some benefits and wisdom medicine gained from experiential equine healing sessions can be increased self-worth and esteem, boosted confidence, decreased anxiety and depression, reduced inflammation, increased self-awareness, and empathy and trust in others and oneself. Finding strength in vulnerability also comes into view when working and being with horses. When we are in nature, all of our senses can come into focus. It is an opportunity to practice letting our masks down in a safe and natural environment, with a profound being we can be certain won't be judging us.

Almost always, there is no riding involved, and there is always a way to invite anyone, no matter the challenge, to enter into an experiential healing session with a horse.

There are several other names you can look for that describe this modality:

- Equine-assisted counseling
- Equine-assisted therapy
- Equine-assisted psychotherapy
- Equine-assisted coaching
- Equine-assisted learning

To get started, you can google any of the above descriptions or simply "horse therapy," to see what facilities or individuals might be offering equine healing in your area.

And in closing, I invite and support you to endeavor the cultivation of social connections. Do not underestimate the damage that self-isolation can inflict, as I have illustrated. It can shorten our lifespan, bring us to the brink of death. Or beyond. The effects are real. Reach out to someone. Let someone know how you are feeling. Staying alone does not help us heal our hearts but instead builds our walls higher and calcifies our hearts. Reach out. You can. You are brave. It is never too late to begin to heal.

I hope you find some of these resources to be useful to you. And please, if you are suffering, ask for help. It can be found. If you would like to contact me, please do. I am available to help you.

Blessings on your healing.

Two palms,

Christin

POEM NOTES

<u>Alphabet</u> page 4

This poem is after *A Is for Annabelle* by Tasha Tudor, my favorite book as a toddler. I credit my mother for my love of books and reading. I would ask her to read it over and over every night before I was satisfied enough to sleep. It sits with its dog ears on my bookshelf in my "beloved" section.

<u>Grandmother</u> page 9

Fear of our human body, its power and beauty, can be directed onto others. In this case, I was the recipient of my grandmother's unconscious projection. It was profoundly wounding and especially confusing for me as a child for two reasons: She was an adult who had authority in my world, and I loved her dearly.

<u>Blue Laces</u> page 16

Anger without recognition, with nowhere to go and no safe outlet, often spurts out in unskillful ways that can be physically scary and damaging. Many times depression is a sign of anger that has been turned back onto oneself. The energy can rise to explosion and crash into collapse. You may recognize these signs in yourself or a loved one.

POEM NOTES

<u>Abuser Erasure</u> page 32

This poem was made using the black-out or erasure technique. This is a copy of one of the many letters I received from this particular abuser. I was fifteen at the time of this letter. This is his handwriting.

<u>Hawk</u> page 40

Yes! This really happened.

<u>Cutter</u> page 63

Hanuman is a Hindu deity who leapt across the ocean to help save a life. This attempted suicide occurred in a dilapidated boardinghouse for transient men, mostly construction workers. There were two floors, seven rooms on each floor, with one shared bathroom for each floor. Women were not allowed. He always snuck me inside. The other men knew I was there and would crack their doors to look at me when he led me by. It was a terrifying place to be. A place I never should have been.

<u>After You Left</u> page 74

It's natural that we try to make meaning. To create narratives offering even a sliver of sense can provide great relief. I am attempting to make sense of what happened to me by asking to understand what may have happened to my mother that could have accounted for her freeze and inability to act.

<u>Grandstand</u> page 80

When my high school was torn down to build a new school, thirty years after I graduated, they left the stadium untouched and intact. It is still there today as it was that day.

POEM NOTES

<u>While Castrating Bull Calves</u> page 89

Often child sexual trauma leads to domestic violence as an adult because appropriate boundaries and self-protective abilities are not instilled as a young person, and often the natural inclination to protect or defend oneself is truncated. Self-esteem, worth, and value can either not develop at all or shatter with abuse and trauma, and this can follow into adulthood. I did not recognize that being taken sexually against my will or being kicked and ridiculed while in the presence of other men constituted abuse or anything out of the ordinary.

<u>Bad Therapy</u> page 99

I did not understand the abject inappropriateness, or lack of ethics, of this kind of "therapy." It was profoundly damaging to hear from this therapist that I must have wanted it. It drove deeper my inherent shame that somehow I brought all of this onto myself. Women can hurt women. Out of ill intent, from the effects of being siloed apart and pitted against one another, or from just plain ignorance.

<u>Height of a Horse Is Measured in Hands</u> page 139

One hand is four inches.

<u>A Chorale of Silence</u> page 142

It was not until 2022 that I told my family the truth of what had happened to me.

<u>What Prevented You from Rescuing Me</u> page 152

Another attempt at understanding how this could have happened to me. My mom was wounded herself, as all of us humans are to some degree; none of us get out of here without getting hurt by life in some sort or shape. She did not have the capacity to protect me and didn't really know why. This speaks to what we can hold so deeply in our unconscious psyche from fear of actually knowing, making it nearly impossible to unearth. Nearly.

And for my fiftieth birthday, Mom baked me the most wonderfully rich carrot cake cupcakes. We laughed and made a toast to breaking the curse of this history and ate this most delicious, sweet healing together.

<u>Wish</u> page 157

When I turned thirty-five years old, I made a private pact with myself that if I still felt all the ways I have described when I turned fifty, I would take my life and end the suffering I could not escape. Frighteningly, it was not until almost the end of my forty-ninth year, and with the completion of this book, that I was able to, and decided to, break my contract and celebrate my healing. On one of my neighborhood walks, while taking a break from working on this manuscript, unbelievably, I found a razor blade. I looked at that blade for a long time when I got home. I understood it was a symbol of the edge I'd lived on and that I had the power to cut and release the invisible cord keeping my past on life support. I could sever the cord, and though there is no forgetting, there can be releasing. Through all of the therapy, all of the healing, all of the horses, all of the writing, the sacred medicine and sisterhood, my determination to heal, never giving up, and simply just all of the excruciating feeling of it all, and finally with the crafting of this book, I learned something. It wasn't that I didn't want to live anymore, it was that I didn't want to live anymore *like this*. And that was the difference.

In this culture, we live with the threat of stigma and shame marking those of us with mental health challenges on any continuum. This shame is unfounded. There is no true origin of it, except fear, and no place for it. To have hearts that shatter and bones that break is human. Let us work together to support all who are hurting. May we be human enough to care. Instead of allowing the pecking death of shame, for those in pain, may we all be brave enough to welcome the full spectrum of all persons of humanity, including our own, and do what it takes to find and offer skillful care. We all deserve to be here, to be seen and to be loved, no matter what pacts we might have secretly made.

<u>Migraine</u> page 165

Purnamadayah is a Sanskrit word meaning "whole, full, or complete."

<u>South Texas Lazarus</u> page 177

A love letter to the landscape I still call home.

<u>It Was Prearranged</u> page 188

The most horrendous validation came for me when this abuser offered no vocal defense or denial. In essence, he confirmed every act with his silence, making everything again very real.

<u>Pancakes</u> page 200

Speaks to the complexity of abusive relationships that contain happiness, easy times, and a sense of normalcy. When good memories are mixed in with memories of abuse, the bind in which the abused child is placed is very real, and the confusion can feel, and be, catastrophic.

<u>The Fifth</u> page 206

When abuse occurs at a preverbal age, before language has developed, the knowing is still contained within the body and can stay lodged there forever, or until it is ready to be known. In a profound state of openness on retreat, I asked the question "What am I ready to know?" The answer came in the shape of this poem. There was one more abuser I hadn't been cognitively aware of. I think maybe I am grateful to my body and mind working in tandem to shield me. This painfully early crossing set the stage and edged me closer toward my own availability to grooming and abuse with zero consciousness of it. It is important to note here that remembering details is not necessary for recovery. The body retains full capacity for healing regardless of memory recall.

POEM NOTES

What If I'd Become a Cherry Clerk page 211

Written after a Saturday-morning coffee tasting at BlendIn Coffee Club, Houston, Texas.

Empty Chair page 242

Empty chair is a well-known Gestalt technique made famous by Fritz Perls in his top-dog/underdog experiments. This technique is often employed in therapy and coaching by non-Gestalt practitioners to great success. Make sure your practitioner is well versed in the skills and nuance of understanding that this technique requires.

A Thousand Tongues page 251

A cut-up of a church bulletin.

Mother, Who We Have Become page 259

Healing and reconciliation do not always happen but are possible. We must be honest, on both sides, and take the courageous risk of becoming vulnerable to own our own personal failings. Willingness to accept the failings of people is also always required.

The word *patriarchy* originates from the Greek word *patriarkhes*, and translates as "the rule of the father." It refers to a social system where men predominantly control a disproportionate share of social, economic, political, and religious power. All people of all genders and orientations feel the effects of this unspoken system today. Especially women.

Patriarchy alienates men from their own feelings and emotions, rendering them into compartmentalized boxes cut off from their innate wholeness. It coerces women to devalue, belittle, and abandon their authenticity in favor of constructed patriarchally sanctioned roles. This strips women of their power and intuitive strength and exiles it into the shadowlands.

It conditions us as women to believe that though we may be victims, we are also, inexplicably, somehow responsible for our own victimization. And because of this, mothers sacrifice their daughters. In some form or fashion. Patriarchy is the origin to this unconsciousness.

My mother is not a monster; she's a victim like me, but of a different realm: generational, cultural, religious, and social. And, like me, is a survivor too.

We must hold people accountable. Period. But in order to do that, as I have read somewhere, we must do a hard thing: We must hold them with our hearts and minds. And that is what I have done with my mom, I have held her.

The return from hell will yield you the life badge of a wounded heart and offer you an anchor into the lotus's mud of compassion and wisdom, and from it you will rise and bloom once more.

The Peony Key page 264

Excerpted verbatim from a five-thousand-word transmission received during a sacred medicine journey. This is how the medicine spoke to me.

Postscript page 297

Bucephalus was the warhorse of Alexander the Great. The bond between this horse and his owner is legendary. His story has reached mythic proportions, and one version is prominently featured in my favorite childhood movie, *The Black Stallion*.

GRATITUDE

Writers do not write alone, even though it may often look and feel that way. Thank you to all writers who have gone before me. You, who have illuminated the way and demonstrated that with craft and courage, it can be done. To all writers who have written with me and at the same time as me. Sometimes at the same shared table. Most often we are strangers stretched across the globe, thank you. To all writers who come after, thank you, and may you, too, reveal your voice and story to us readers, who will always be ready to receive you, learn from you, and to remind you that you are not alone.

To *National Geographic* award-winning photographer Rodney Bursiel, of Wimberley, Texas, thank you for your willingness to allow one of your timeless photographs to add its grace and power to the cover of my book. I needed an image that could provide an anchor and serve as the container to hold my words, and this horse clearly does just that.

To Mark Gelotte, for your original vision that led to this stunning cover, and Cass Miosic, for your early editorial support, thank you!

Becky Jordan, I am grateful to you for connecting Rodney and me. Thank you, girlfriend, for your friendship. Our conversations helped me through some difficult stages near the end of this journey. Greg, your feedback from a masculine perspective was powerful for me. Thank you.

GRATITUDE

Thank you to my dear friend Susie Peebler, your cheerleading and uplifting "atta girls!" are the best! Our friendship is the rare and precious gem of reciprocity, presence, trust, and love.

To Pam Stockton, who graciously agreed to peer-read this manuscript with her therapeutic eyes, I am grateful for the generosity of your spirit, time, and insightful comments on this collection. Your clean and open heart coupled with your keen, razor-sharp mind is a mighty combination, which this collection drew great merit from. And so have I. Pam, thank you for your guidance, love, and sisterhood. OX.

Amy K. Musson, what can I say about you? Awesomesauce growth and leadership coach, host of the podcast *The Growth Moment*, compassionate intuitive woman, fearless mama-bear mother, skillful reader, and dear friend. For all the hours and hours you spent with me, on my manuscript and otherwise, with your gentle heart and open ear, asking the perfect laser questions at just the right moments, I thank you and love you.

To Karen Upson and the rock-and-roll team at Girl Friday Productions for your enthusiasm and expert implementation of your craft that allowed this book to be born into this world, thank you! And an extra special shout-out to Abi Pollokoff!

Dear family, we have been on a challenging yet tight-knit life journey together. Thank you for being who you are. I love you all, each one, and feel the reciprocity. Let's keep the storytelling-at-supper tradition alive.

Dear Mom, I forgive you. Thank you for understanding that I had to write this story for my own salvation, and for bravely and selflessly supporting me to do it despite knowing how hard it would be for you. I love you so much. We have marvelous adventures ahead. Life is short, let's saddle up!

Dear Dad, I love you exactly as you are.

GRATITUDE

To Russ and Larrine Abolt, my much-loved fairy godparents. You have been riding this healing journey with me for decades, and your constant support and love has made a sweeping difference in my life. Thank you.

To the regal and humble priestess Diane Haug, thank you for your mentorship and friendship. And for the candlelight scribing.

To my dear Irish auntie, Nancy Killorin, who was there for me during the writing of this book, when I felt most alone. I will never forget this. I love you. Thank you.

To my canine constant companion, Lali, you are always, always, by my side. Thank you, dear daughter dog, for your comfort, attention, and loyalty beyond compare.

For all of the equines on this planet and beyond, and especially to my horses, thank you for your wisdom and patience. You are my medicine.

To each and every one of my clients, you have unbeknownst assisted, insisted, and supported me to continue my own healing journey. It is my great passion, purpose, and honor to be in service to you, and as witness to your transformations, I bow. Thank you.

My dearest Dana. Neither this book nor my recovery could have happened without you. For all that you have endured with me, I'm sorry. Forgive me. Thank you. I love you. For always.

Child of Eve, rattle the apple tree!

—The Light Rider

ABOUT THE AUTHOR

Christin Marie Staszesky is a Gestaltist, somatic practitioner, yogi, poet, memoirist, oneironaut (one who studies the interpretation of dreams), lifetime horse listener, and equine wisdom weaver. In this lifetime, she lives as The Light Rider, her personal archetypal myth.

Her trauma-informed private practice in Houston, Texas, fuses the creativity of Gestalt psychology, co-active coaching, and polyvagal neurobiology with soma-centered intelligence, body language, therapeutics, and modalities.

Christin brings to her practice forty-five years' worth of equine medicine gifts and over three decades of study as both a teacher and student of yoga. She also facilitates Principle-Based Partner Yoga™.

She is a graduate of the Innate Somatic Intelligence Trauma Therapy Approach, developed by Manuela Mischke-Reeds, and is a continual student of many traditions of dreamwork.

Christin offers private and group sessions to individuals, couples, and families. She hosts workshops and retreats synthesizing Gestalt, horses, writing, and yoga.

ABOUT THE AUTHOR

When not with clients, she delights in green-tea parties, beachcombing, stargazing, witching in the kitchen, dancing, hiking, and full-moon forest bathing.

Christin feels most at home on a horse. And her magic wand, the pen, is always in her back pocket.

thelightrider.com

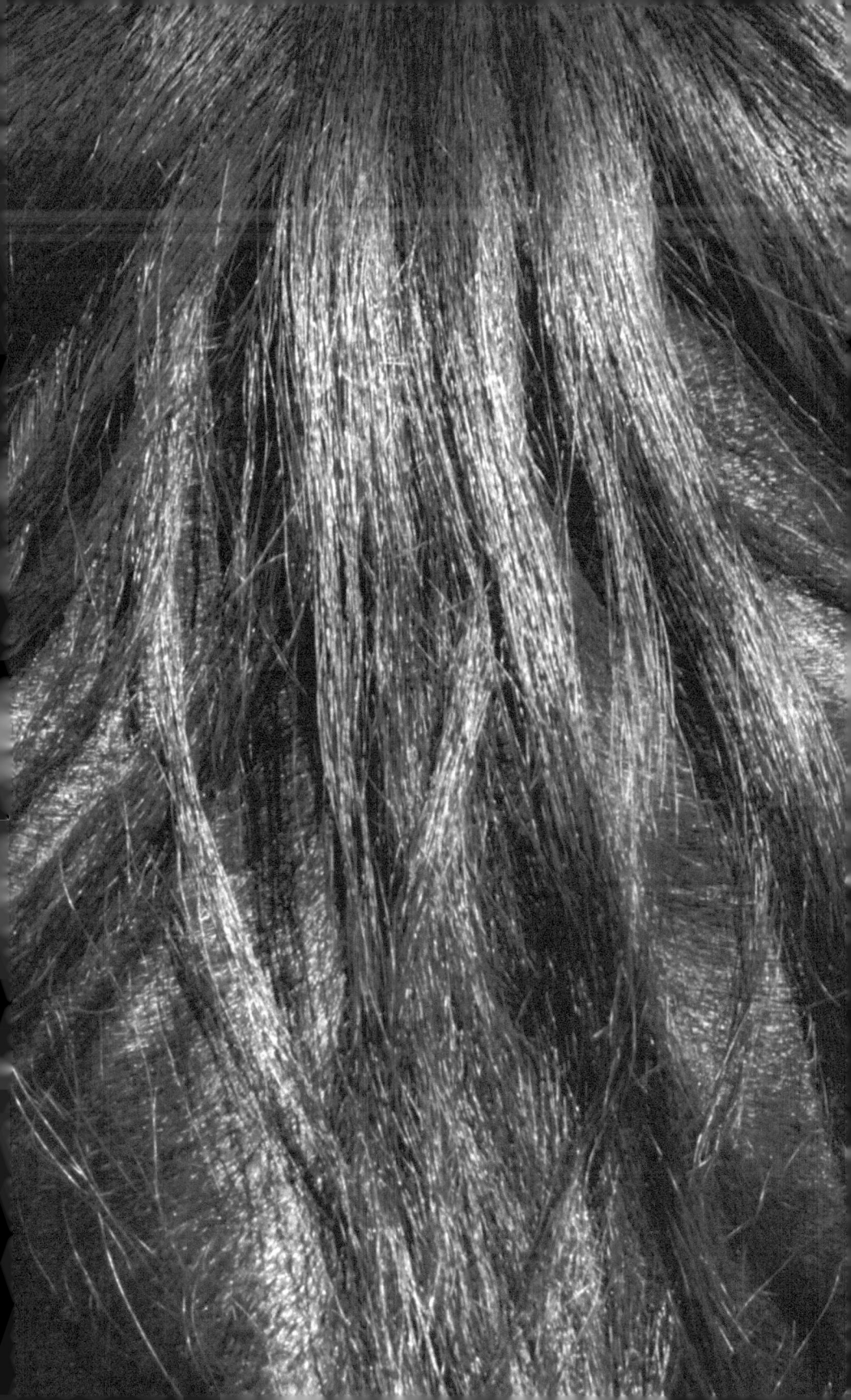

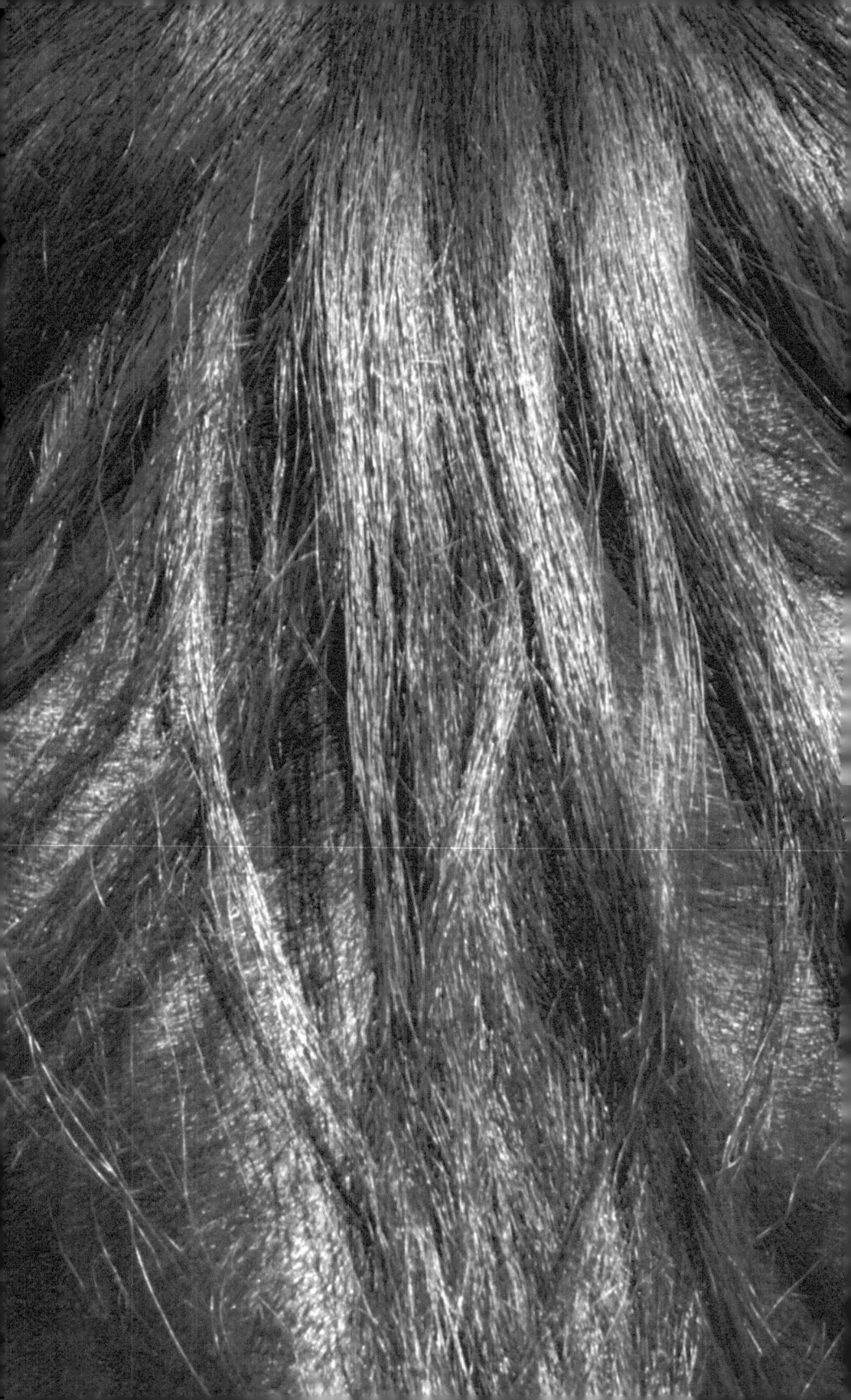